Made for the Country

Made for the Country

ROBERT KIMBER

Lyons & Burford, Publishers

With the exception of "Tools for Taming the Wild Side" (Scythes and Sickles) and "Carts and Barrows," which first appeared in *Horticulture,* all the pieces here were originally published as "Made for the Country" columns in *Country Journal* Magazine. Both the columns and the column name are used with permission.

Printed in the United States of America

10 9 8 7 6 5 4 3 2 1

Library of Congress Cataloging-in-Publication Data

Kimber, Robert.
Made for the country / Robert Kimber.
p. cm.
ISBN 1-55821-103-9 : $17.95
1. Home economics, Rural. 2. Country life. I. Title.
TX147.K54 1991
640'.9173'4—dc20 90-29043
CIP

❧ For RITA

Contents

Preface

Except for "Carts and Barrows" and "Tools for Taming the Wild Side," which first appeared in *Horticulture: The Magazine of American Gardening*, all of the pieces collected here were written as "Made for the Country" columns in *Country Journal*. When I started writing this column four years ago, I had the privilege that all fresh starts bestow: I could write the rules. Not surprisingly, those rules turned out to be a codification of my own biases as a consumer, and I assumed that most readers of *Country Journal*, when they went out to buy tools, clothing, or any kind of gear for country living, would be looking for the same qualities I did. They would not want to buy anything that was environmentally harmful either in its application or in its manufacture. They would prefer soft technology over hard. They would favor products that increase self-sufficiency and encourage the use of renewable resources. They would want to know if a new product or material represented a real advance over the old. Did it do what it said it did? Was it rugged, durable, and economical? Or was the old standby still the best choice? In short, what I wanted to do—and what I assumed most readers would want me to do—was provide information that would help them make thoughtful, budget-minded purchases. The column would not be a parade ground for any and every new item to come on the market. It would not ask simply what new things are there to buy but rather what things do country dwellers truly need, for work and for play, and what products, new or old, best meet those needs.

For answers to those questions I've drawn largely on my own experience of living and working on an old farm in northwestern Maine where my wife and I have kept a kitchen garden, raised chickens, ducks, and sheep, heated with wood, restored an ancient farmhouse, and sought many of our pleasures in the woods and on the mountains and waterways of Maine. That does not mean, however, that I've regarded the column as a chance simply to pontificate and tell everybody what my own august preferences are. I've tried to research each topic carefully, analyze the strengths and weaknesses of competing products, and be clear about my reasons when I have made judgments. Similarly, I have not let my basic preference for natural materials over synthetics blind me to the virtues of synthetics. There are many products—rope, for instance—in which synthetics are plainly superior. There are still others, such as cross-country skis, in which the natural material (wood) is better for some conditions, the synthetics for others.

Finally, in addition to providing full information about products and fair-minded assessments of them, I wanted to enjoy writing these columns, and I wanted people to enjoy reading them, whether they happened to be in the market for tire chains or a garden hose at the moment or not. So I've allowed myself what some might consider frivolous digressions into such weighty matters as the history and natural history of brooms and hammocks.

Prices, models, model names, and whole lines of products change rapidly; companies move and go out of business. The information of that kind given here was current at the time each column was written. If any details are no longer correct, I apologize for these ravages of time but feel there is little point in updating information that is subject to constant change. The essentials will, I hope, remain valid.

My last words here are words of thanks, first, to David Sleeper for welcoming me to *Country Journal* some eight years ago and then, as managing editor, offering me the "Made for the Country" column; to Paul Schullery, who edited the column for many months with a discerning eye and a gentle hand and always had something funny to tell me on the phone; to Peter Fossel for the fresh energy and thinking he has brought to *Country Journal* with his editorship; and to Nick Lyons and Peter Burford for giving all these pieces a good home together under one roof.

HOME AND HEARTH

A Clean Sweep

A new broom *does* sweep clean; and if you think about it for a minute (which I have never bothered to do until now), you'll hit on a few good reasons why.

The fiber used in a good household broom comes from broomcorn, which is not corn at all but a variety of sorghum. Although the plant looks like corn, its seed grows not in ears but in the tassels of strawlike fibers at the top of the stalks. Each tassel may have 60 to 100 straws, and the tips of the individual straws are further subdivided into fine, seed-bearing fibers. If you look closely at a broom head, you'll see that the straws at the shoulders of the broom and down past the stitching are smooth but that the lower five or six inches branch out into those fine fibers. And if you put those fibers under a microscope, you'll see that they, in turn, have minute spurs on them. It is those small fibers and the hairlike spurs that catch and hold even very fine dust.

As the broom ages and wears down, losing an inch, then two and three inches, more and more of those dirt-grabbing fibers are lost until only the coarse upper fibers are left and the surface area and flexibility of the broom are reduced. When the broom is new, it flexes and spreads over a wide area. Each stroke of the broom brings the largest possible number of broomcorn hairlets in contact with the widest possible swath of dirty floor. And so it is that a new broom sweeps clean.

The upright broom has not changed much in its basic shape since 1798, the year when Brother Theodore Bates of the Shaker community in Watervliet, New York, invented the flat broom to replace the age-old but hopelessly inefficient round one. Bates' invention launched one of the Shakers' major industries, and the Pleasant Hill community in Kentucky is said to have produced up to 50,000 brooms in one year. But important as the broom was in the Shakers' commercial life, it was even more important to their spiritual life. Indeed, cleanliness and godliness were so closely linked for the Shakers that their worship services included what they called the "sweeping gift," a symbolic pantomime in which the Brothers and Sisters would sweep the meetinghouse floor with imaginary brooms as they sang lines like

Sweep sweep and cleanse your floor
Mother's standing at the door.

"Mother" was not your mother or mine but Mother Ann, the founder of Shakerism, who had instructed her followers to "sweep clean the floor of the heart."

In *The Housewares Story: A History of the American Housewares Industry* (Chicago: National Housewares Manufacturers Association, 1973), the author tells us that "the broom was no match for that remarkable newcomer, the vacuum cleaner, and as cleaner sales increased broom sales declined." Well, maybe so, but I can't imagine sweeping the floor of my heart clean with a vacuum cleaner, nor can I imagine a rural household functioning very well without a broom. Who is going to get out a vacuum cleaner every time the kids come stomping through, shedding leaves, pine needles, and corrugated mud from their sneakers?

Broomcorn is as good a material today as it ever was, and the best household brooms are made of 100 percent broomcorn, as are many heavier weight janitorial and industrial brooms meant for sweeping fine dirt. Upright brooms may differ greatly in size and weight, but they differ very little in construction. The corn is moistened to make it pliable before it is wound onto the broom handle with wire. The broom is then clamped in a shaping mold and stitched with three to five rows of stitching. Winding and stitching are still done by hand, so a good broom depends both on the quality of the materials and the skill of the broom maker.

When you select a broom look at the tip to see that the fibers split off into the tiny "flags" of genuine broom corn. Barn brooms and some other heavy-duty brooms may either contain—or be made entirely of—rattan or other coarse natural fibers to make the broom stiffer and able to handle heavier dirt. Yucca and sotol are also used as fillers in low- and medium-priced kitchen and household brooms, but because these fibers do not have the flags of broomcorn, they make much less efficient sweepers.

Broomcorn is a clear, greenish yellow in color. If you want a dyed broom, you can still tell by looking at the fiber tips whether it is all, or only partially, broomcorn. Rely on your own eyes and hands rather than on labels when you select a broom. The words "corn" or "natural fibers" in a label are generic and indicate only that you will be getting some kind of natural fiber. Vining Industries' Item 108, for example, sells for $6.99 in my local grocery store and is labeled a "Natural Corn Broom." The core is what I take to be sotol while the outside "skirt" is broom corn, so this particular broom is indeed "natural" and "corn" but not *all* broomcorn. Only brooms that are "100-per-cent broomcorn" can use that phrase in the label. But even then there can be some variation in the grade. Look and feel. The more fine end fibers there are, the better the broom, and the cleaner the sweep.

The handle is also a key to quality. Is its diameter proportional to the size of the head and therefore heavy enough to do the work required of it? Is it cracked or rough? Does a coat of paint slopped on it cover a multitude of sins? I always prefer a handle with a clear lacquer finish so that I can see the grain of the wood.

Look at the workmanship. A cheap broom is clearly just a round broom whose lower quarters have been squashed flat and sewn in place. A better broom has carefully molded and flattened shoulders that are firm and smooth. There should be no bulges or lumps indicating bunched or crumpled fibers inside. Is the broomcorn thick and even, or are there gaps or thin spots? The broom head should be symmetrical, not lopsided or askew.

Stitching should be snug and straight with a stitch roughly every half inch. The number of rows of stitching will depend on the size of the broom. A good wound broom will ordinarily have a minimum of four rows; longer, heavier models will have five or six. A light kitchenette broom, such as Hamburg's "Sweepy" or Vining's "Extra Lite," in which the fibers are seated in a metal cap, may have only two or three. The wire winding at the throat should be neat and even without stray fibers sticking out of it.

Finally, a good broom will feel good in the hands. It will have the heft, balance, and authority that any well-made tool has. Most of the "bargain" brooms you can pick up for anywhere from $3 to $7 in grocery and discount stores fail all of the above tests. A broom that passes them all with flying colors, however, is the "No. 7 Puritan" made by the Hamburg Broom Works, Inc., of Hamburg, Pennsylvania. This is a 100 percent broomcorn broom that measures 16½ inches from tip to shoulder, is beautifully finished in every detail, and costs $9.49 at our local Farmers Union. A broom of this size is big enough to handle a large country kitchen and rugged enough to do light outdoor chores, such as sweeping fluffy snow off the porch. When it wears down a couple of inches, we continue to use it in garage, woodshed, and ell, and buy a new one for the kitchen.

Hamburg's principal market area is in the Northeast. If you live somewhere else, don't be discouraged. Look at the top line offered by the companies that market in your area, like the "Premium Household Broom" (also about $9.50) made by Lorenz Housewares, Inc., of Newbury Park, California. And remember that all broomcorn brooms are fashioned from a natural material by human hands. Each one is a little different from the next. Half the fun is picking out the prettiest broom in the rack.

A surefire way to get an ugly broom is to buy a plastic one. Let me be brief about plastic brooms: I think they're crummy, even though they now account for about a quarter to a third of the brooms sold annually in this country. The tips of synthetic bristles are extruded to form many tiny flags to imitate the natural hairs of broom corn and so be able to pick up fine dust. And the manufacturers will tell you that because synthetic bristles are uniform, there is a consistency in plastic brooms that corn brooms, made of variable materials by inconsistent human hands, can't have. One plastic broom is exactly like the next one. So who needs a consistently poor product? Plastic bristles do not have the pliability of natural fibers, and using a plastic broom is more like stabbing and swatting than sweeping. Dirt does indeed cling to a plastic broom, and it will soon be a foul, greasy mess. Granted, it can be washed, but I don't want to spend my time washing brooms. Finally, the balance, shape, and construction of plastic brooms are insults to the hand and eye. Ugly to look at, wretched to hold, they finally make their way to the dump where they will be with us for all time.

The reasons why plastic is making inroads on broomcorn are cost and availability. Making natural-fiber brooms remains a labor-intensive craft. People still wind the fiber onto the handle; people still do the stitching. Growing broomcorn is expensive, too, because it has to be hand harvested; and most of the broomcorn used in this country today is imported from Mexico, where labor is much cheaper. This double dependence on skilled labor and on imported raw materials accounts for the rise of the plastic broom.

But for as long as there are broomcorn brooms around, I will sweep with them; and once I've got a pile of dirt together, I'll pick it up with the world's most practical dust pan: Fuller Brush's Metal Dust Pan, Item Number 863, selling for about $6.50. This simply designed pan with its thin, slightly beveled pick-up edges slithers under dirt and doesn't make you keep chasing yourself backwards around the kitchen floor trying to pick up that last thin line of dust. There is a matching Stair Brush, Item No. 329, for about $7.00, to which my only objection is that the bristles are now synthetic rather than horsehair. If you can't chase down a Fuller Brush representative in your phone book, call or write The Fuller Brush Company, 2800 Rockcreek Parkway, Suite 400, North Kansas City, Missouri 64117, 816-474-1754.

Home Haircuts

Country living has always called for a certain measure of self-sufficiency; but about fifteen years ago when young and not so young folks began moving to the country in droves, self-sufficiency was elevated from a useful virtue to an article of faith. Among the many skills I took a whack at in those days was cutting my own hair. If, I thought, I can churn butter; grow, thresh, and winnow wheat and rye; raise and butcher sheep; put sills under an ancient farm house; keep aging automobiles and tractors alive; and so on and on, then I ought to be able to lop off a few locks of hair. I was right. I could.

In the meantime, I've come to appreciate the virtues of specialization. It's nice to be able to do just about anything yourself, but it's even nicer to not have to. I've retired the butter churn and the flail, for instance, but not my barber's scissors. In my periodic re-evaluations of what it makes sense for me to do or not do myself, haircutting has always kept a solid place in the will-do column.

There are a number of good reasons for a country dweller to take up home haircutting, one of the most compelling being re moteness from a professional barber or beautician. At one point in my fairly distant past if I had wanted the services of a professional barber in February, I would have had to snowshoe a mile and half and drive twelve more on Tuesday only, the one day a week when the itinerant barber of northwestern Maine happened to be in town. Nowadays, even in the dead of winter, I can forgo the snowshoes and drive only six miles any workday of the week.

Even though I can no longer offer great distance, arduous travel, and complicated logistics as part of my rationale for home barbering, I can certainly still offer efficiency and economy. In my own bathroom, I can get a haircut when I want it. I do not have to sit around for half an hour, reading a coverless issue of *Sports Afield* (June 1978) while I wait my turn. And at home I save $5 a shot. In a year that's roughly $50, maybe more. For two heads of hair, it's $100; for three, $150. Before too long, your home haircuts can buy you a new fly rod.

But far heavier on my scale of values than hours and dollars saved is the torment I am spared. At home, I do not get a tight little paper collar wound around my neck; I do not have to tell the barber precisely what I want, then argue with him when he does precisely what he pleases; I do not have to inhale clouds of talcum powder; I do not have to spend the rest of my day squirming and scratching as the debris of my haircut makes its way down my neck, back, and belly. At home, I can strip naked, let the fur fly, and—when I'm done—step from mirror to shower to wash the whole itchy, creepy, crawly mess away.

Now I should warn you that among some folks in the barbering and hairdressing trade, this kind of talk is outright heresy. They want you to believe that cutting hair is something like brain surgery: If amateurs try it, they'll mess up their heads irreversibly and for all time. Patently untrue. As one home haircutter of my acquaintance pointed out, the difference between a bad haircut and a good one is about three days. Take comfort in that. No matter how badly you botch the job, nature will give you a chance to do better next time.

Less defensive professional haircutters, while taking justifiable pride in their skills, will not try to veil their work in unwarranted mystery. Such a man is Bob Bent, the author of a book called *How to Cut Your Own or Anybody Else's Hair* (New York: Simon and Schuster, 1975), $8.95. Bent provides simple, straightforward instructions for basic haircuts for men and women—the short cut, layered cut, long cut, and one-length cut—as well as cuts for children. Step-by-step illustrations make it easy to visualize the process as you go along. His advice on hair care is as sensible as his instructions on cutting it: Wash it frequently with natural, nondetergent shampoo; keep chemicals and heat away from it. He does not go so far as to condemn permanents, rinses, curling, and straightening outright, but it's quite clear where his sympathies lie. "Generally," he says, "I feel that hair should be left alone to grow as it will. Healthy, natural hair looks best—if it's cut properly." His approach of cultivating healthy hair and then choosing a style of cut that suits your face, build, and hair makes the best kind of sense for anyone living an outdoor, rural life.

Another good book is *Cutting Hair at Home* by Patricia Bozic and Lee Pola (New York: New American Library, 1986), $8.95. This one covers more ground than Bent's, offering a number of haircutting tips, more ideas on choosing a hair style (mainly for women), and a section on home permanents and hair coloring. I find Bent's haircutting directions and illustrations more lucid and easier to follow, Bozic and Pola's, more detailed but also fussier and less cogent. A licensed beautician who started out cutting her family's hair at home said she found going by a book very helpful to her at first, but she also stressed to me the importance not only of knowledge but of mental and emotional tools—relaxation, confidence, taking it easy, and taking your time.

The basic physical tools—scissors and a comb—are so simple that they would hardly seem to require comment. The comb doesn't. You can buy a straight, narrow barber's comb about a half-inch wide and with fine and coarse teeth in any drugstore. The advantage of that shape is that it picks up smaller wads of hair. (Remember? Take your time.) Drugstores also carry barber scissors. The ones I found in my local stores were all seven-inch models and ran from about $6 to $12. They will do, but they're not great. Shorter scissors are lighter and give you more control. Four and a half to 5½ inches is a good length. Good professional haircutting scissors will pivot easily on the center screw and not bind at all. They'll be much sharper than your kitchen-drawer shears; they'll hold their edge longer; and they'll be made of nonrusting stainless steel.

The few barber- and beauty-supply dealers I spoke to do not sell to anyone but professionals. (One clerk fixed me with an icy stare and said, "We do not condone home haircutting.") So unless you have better luck than I did, you may not be able to locate professional-quality barber shears easily. One possible source is a good cutlery shop, if there is one near you. And one sure source is E. M. Geib, Jr., 1311 Gladiolas Drive, Winter Park, Florida 32792. Ed Geib sells an excellent line of haircutting scissors called "Buttercut," and he will take mail or phone orders. He suggests you call him at 305- 678-8023 and talk over with him exactly what you want. Scissors he offers the home haircutter range from $24 to $40, obviously a lot more than the drugstore variety, but you should have a tool that will give you a lifetime of trouble-free service.

Add to your scissors and comb a couple of long metal hair clips, which you use to keep one section of hair out of the way while you're working on another, and your kit is complete. I have never used electric clippers, and neither of the two books mentioned above even acknowledges their existence. But if you want to do buzz cuts or some mowing around the ears and on the back of your head, you can buy clippers from mail-order sources. Sears has a barber's kit that includes electric clippers, cleaning brush, oil, five snap-on cutting attachments, scissors, two combs, and a cape for $19.99. The clipper set alone costs $14.99. Sears also has a professional-grade Oster clipper for $79.99. Brookstone, 127 Vose Farm Road, Peterborough, New Hampshire 03460, 603-924-9541, and Leichtung, Inc., 4944 Commerce Parkway, Cleveland, Ohio 44128, 800-321-6840, both offer a complete barber's kit, with a Wahl clipper, for about $37.

Sweeping Out the Soot

The first advice I got on cleaning chimneys came from an earlier age, and no wonder. Dana Hamlin, the man I asked for that advice, was ninety-three years old. Dana suggested I take a small spruce tree, tie ropes to either end of it, and yank it up and down the chimney. With its tough, springy branches trimmed to make a snug fit in the flue, a young spruce will in fact do a fair job of cleaning your chimney. But Lord, what a production: Cut the tree, trim the tree, tie ropes to it, persuade your mate to pull it down through the chimney while you stand on the roof to pull it up. The system was not conducive to the frequent cleanings I like to give my chimneys; and so, mumbling my due respects to spruce trees, I bought a chimney brush.

The Worcester Brush Company, the leading U.S. manufacturer of chimney brushes both in quality and in volume of sales, offers a homeowner line called "Professional's Choice," and a professional sweep's line called "Master Sweep." The Pro's Choice, which is not in fact the professional grade, is the brush you're likely to find in hardware stores and farmers' unions. Suggested retail on the 7-by-7-inch size I need is about $20. For $3 or $4 more, you can buy the same size in Master Sweep, though you will probably not find it in the hardware store and will have to special order it from a fireplace and woodstove store. The extra trouble and the few extra dollars are, in my mind, well spent. Though both grades use the same alloy wire, the Master Sweep has almost three times as many bristles. They not only add to durability but also vastly improve the cleaning action.

Even stiffer than the Master Sweep is the flat wire brush, which professional sweeps use to attack accumulations of gooey creosote. Price for a Worcester 7-by-7: about $33, though my local woodstove shop sells an excellent "Sweep's Choice" flat-wire brush made by Wood-Fuel Technology, Ltd., Bridgewater, Nova Scotia, for only $24. If you clean your chimney regularly and burn well-seasoned wood, you may feel you have no need for this heavy-duty brush. But it is such an efficient tool that I have taken to using it for my routine cleaning.

My assumption thus far has been that you are a woodburner and will therefore use a metal-bristle brush. Metal brushes can be used safely not only in masonry chimneys but also in insulated steel pre-fab chimneys listed by Underwriters Laboratories. If you burn coal or oil, use brushes with polypropylene bristles because the acids in these flues will quickly deteriorate metal bristles. Also, I have read that metal brushes (and rods with steel fittings) can spark fires in coal flues. I have no experience with coal flues and cannot tell you how serious or common this problem is. A 7-by-7-inch poly brush costs about $16.

The brush size should match the *inside* measurements of your flue. A 7-by-7-inch flue takes a 7-by-7-inch brush. This exact match is particularly important with stiff brushes (flat-wire or Master Sweep) and small flues. If you're using a softer brush (Pro's Choice) in a large flue, a brush that is a half inch or even an inch oversize will not get hung up or exert so much pressure that it damages the flue.

You can get by with a brush alone, attaching ropes to either end of it, as I used to with my spruce tree. But the rope system has its obvious drawbacks. It takes two people instead of one (unless you are willing to scramble repeatedly from roof to cellar and cellar to roof to yank the brush down, then up, and so forth), and it is difficult, if not impossible, to scrub away at one short section of the flue. Extension rods are much easier and more efficient. You screw the brush onto your first rod section, stuff the brush down the flue, screw on another section, and so on. If you see a particularly dirty section of chimney, you can work the brush up and down through it several times.

In chimney-cleaning rods, fiberglass is the standard material. For my needs (working from the roof down on perfectly straight flues), I prefer the professional grade to the light duty one. Known as 3/8-inch (by the thread size of the fittings), rods of this size are large enough in diameter to give you something to hold onto and rugged enough to let you punch through tight spots. They come in 4-, 5-, and 6-foot lengths. Worcester four-footers retail for about $8 apiece. Longer lengths are cheaper per foot but a little more awkward to handle. If you have a flue with major bends in it, the thinner, 1/4-inch rods will flex enough to do the job; and that is why every professional sweep has a set of them in his kit. Another alternative is the Euro-Pro rod. Equipped with nonsparking brass fittings, this rod is so durable and flexible that it can be run up through clean-out doors without risk of breaking. Professional sweeps like it because it lets them work indoors and with their feet on the ground. But for the homeowner who cleans three chimneys a year, not three chimneys a day, the price is high (about $8 per 3-foot section).

Rods and brushes are your basic tools, something like toothpaste and toothbrush for your teeth. But if you want to floss as well, use one of the manganese-salt chimney cleaners, available in granulated or liquid form, as part of your regular chimney maintenance (Safe-T-Flue, about $9 for two pounds; Anti-Creo-Soot and Liquid Safe-T-Flue, both about $11 per quart). The liquids are much easier to use. The manganese salts act as a catalyst to loosen creosote, preventing buildup and helping you get rid of it if you have some. These products are irritating to the eyes and mucous membranes and should be used and stored with the same care appropriate for any industrial chemical. However, they are much more effective and safer to use than the chemical cleaners that use sodium chloride and copper sulphate or trisodium phosphate. These cleaners are not only toxic and irritating to eyes and skin, but they also corrode both metal and masonry.

You want to have your chimneys clean in the fall, right before the heavy heating season sets in, but it's just as important to clean your whole heating system in the spring. Soot and ash soak up moisture in the spring and summer and create acids damaging to metal and masonry. Coal-burning systems are particularly vulnerable. Two good chimney cleanings a year—fall and spring—seem the absolute minimum to me, and my conscience is never completely at rest unless I've seized a moderately warm and wind-still January day to give my chimneys a midwinter reaming as well.

Safety and Cleanliness

The home chimney sweep does not need the high-powered safety gear that a professional who spends his or her entire working life in clouds of soot needs to have, but there are a few essentials that even the two-or-three-times-a-year sweep should not be without.

At the top of the list is a respirator. Soot and the vapors released during chimney cleaning are carcinogens, and you want to keep them out of your own pipes. A surgeon's mask or wet bandanna is the absolute minimum. Neither is snug fitting or fine enough for my tastes, and I use a dust/mist respirator that covers nose and mouth with a rubber face mask and has a single filter (about $11 from Sears). A step up is the Comfo II, which has two dust filters plus a charcoal vapor filter (about $37) and is the minimal protection for a professional sweep.

I also wear my shop goggles, which are contoured to fit the head and have a soft plastic rim. Goggles of this kind cost about $4, and Sears has dust and chemical goggles for about the same price. A sweep's model with a double, nonfogging lens and a tight foam seal costs about $33. A cap that covers your ears completes your headgear.

Chimneys, thimbles, stovepipe, and wire brushes (not to mention fiberglass slivers from battered rods) can take a bloody toll on your hands if you don't wear sturdy leather work gloves.

Last but far from least is firm footing if you're working on the roof. Use a ladder and ridge hook or a light, portable scaffolding. If you use a safety rope, don't tie it to the chimney—an old rotten one could very well come down on top of you.

To prevent soot from getting into the house, tape a drop cloth or sheet of plastic over the fireplace and any other openings into the living area. If you're working from below, leave a hole in the plastic to run your rod through.

All the experts warn against using your home vacuum cleaner to pick up soot. The stuff is so fine that it can get through the bag and damage the motor. I confess I did not know this until recently and have been putting our ancient Kenmore at risk of its life for years.

When you're all done, throw your clothes in a washtub to soak, and take a long, hot shower. You'll have earned it.

Oil Lamps

We may like to think winter is on its way out in March, but this is the time of year when gale-force winds and heavy, wet snows are most likely to take out power lines. When that happens, you grab your flashlight, but what do you grab next? Candles are great fun for a festive dinner, but for an extended power outage you'll want something that burns longer, brighter, and more steadily than a candle. Oil lamps were standard equipment in rural households well into this century, and though electricity may have dimmed their sales, they remain a boon to a blacked-out home, and they are still the main source of artificial light in parts of the world beyond the reach of utility lines.

Pressurized mantle lanterns that use highly volatile fuels like white gas or Coleman fuel put out a lot of light, but I think of them as outdoor—not indoor—lighting. They are hot and noisy, and a volatile fuel under pressure near rugs, curtains, and finished table tops makes me nervous. In short, I don't want a gas lantern at the dinner table.

Oil lamps are better suited to indoor use. Although any open flame represents a fire hazard, oil is not volatile, and in lamps it is not under pressure. Also, oil lamps are quiet, and because they are a household furnishing rather than an outdoor implement, they blend into and enhance an indoor setting.

Illumination in an oil lamp comes from a flat wick, a round wick, or an incandescent mantle. I've seen wick lamps described as "liquid-fueled candles with bigger wicks." That may describe how the lamp functions and the type of light it supplies, but it downplays some important differences. For one, an oil lamp does not consume itself or its wick as it burns. The oil burns; the wick does not. Wicks have to be trimmed now and then to remove carbon deposits, but a properly tended wick will last for many years of occasional use and for quite a few of heavy use. Because the lamp's flame is protected by a glass chimney, it takes a heavy draft to set it flickering; and the airflow created by the burner and chimney design produces a wide, fan-shaped flame rather than a pointed one.

But for all that, a flat-wick lamp still does not produce a stunning amount of light. Flat wicks come in widths from ¼-inch to as much as 2⅝-inches with ¾- or ⅞-inch being the most common household sizes. Folks in the oil-lamp business estimate the illumination of an oil lamp with a ⅞-inch wick at about six to twelve candlepower. The larger the wick, the more light; and one way to increase the burning surface without having to have an excessively wide burner to accommodate a huge wick is to bend a flat wick into the form of a tube. This design, by providing a central draft tube, delivers more oxygen to the flame and so helps it burn brighter. But even with these improvements, tubular-wick lamps barely double the output of a flat-wick lamp. Miniature oil lamps that use solid round wicks not much larger than candlewicks are truly just liquid-fueled candles, and they produce even less light than flat-wick lamps.

The only oil lamp that provides the white, bright light you'll want for reading or fine needlework is the Aladdin mantle lamp. It works on the same principle used in pressurized gas lanterns. The flame in the lamp does not produce the light directly but instead heats a rayon mantle to the point of incandescence. In a gas lantern, the flame is fueled with vaporized gasoline. In the Aladdin mantle lamp, a round wick delivers the oil and hence the flame right under the mantle. Aladdin lamps produce light equivalent to a 60-watt bulb. That's at least four times the light of a round-wick lamp and anywhere from six to ten times the light of flat-wick lamps.

Incandescent mantles are impregnated with cesium and naturally radioactive thorium. Aladdin spokesman Bill Webb says that tests indicate no physical danger from exposure to this extremely low level of radiation. To be on the safe side, however, Aladdin provides safety tips for handling and disposing of mantles.

Flat-wick lamps are inexpensive, costing roughly between $5 and $15. Aladdins are the most expensive oil lamps, ranging from a suggested retail price of $40.50 for the basic Genie to upwards of $100 for the fancier models. The burners are identical in all the Aladdins, so you get the same light no matter which one you buy. The options in font design and material (brass, aluminum, or glass) and in the type of shade (paper or hand-painted glass) account for the wide range of prices. Round-wick lamps (Aladdin makes these, too) cost nearly as much as the basic Aladdin mantle lamps. Suggested retail on Aladdin's "Black-Out Kit," which includes a round-wick lamp for either table or wall-bracket use plus a quart of oil, is $33.

The slightly brighter light provided by tubular, round-wick lamps is not enough of an improvement over flat wicks to justify the much higher price. If you are interested solely in lighting for power outages, buy a couple of cheap flat-wick lamps to help you find your way around the house and add an Aladdin mantle lamp so that you can read comfortably. If you experience frequent and extended power outages or if you are equipping a home that will have neither electric nor gas lighting, then each family member should be issued an Aladdin.

The Aladdin Genie is cheap because it uses an inexpensive glass font and has no shade. From a purely utilitarian point of view, the Aluminum Shelf Lamp with a white shade (Model B139S, suggested retail $77) is worth the extra money. A shade is essential for comfortable use of the lamp, and the font of this lamp is mounted on a low pedestal that makes it easy to carry the lamp securely in one hand. If you want more elegance, choose one of the similarly designed brass models with glass shades. Metal fonts have the advantage of being unbreakable and the disadvantage that you can't see when they need refilling.

With flat-wick lamps, too, I prefer models that can be carried easily and securely. The most practical designs have a candlestick-style fingerhold. Lamplight Farms' Chamber model with a glass font and fingerhold lists for $8. Lamplight Farms also offers a number of other styles with larger, more ornate fonts, for example: the Bordeaux, $17; the Fire and Ice, $11.50.

How well your lamps perform will depend on what you burn in them and how you operate them. The more highly refined the oil, the less odor and smoke you will get. Lamplight Farms Ultra-Pure is an extremely clean-burning oil (suggested retail: $3.50 per quart; $12 per gallon) that leaves no odor even if several lamps are burning in the same room. A less expensive oil perfectly suitable for home use is Lamplight Farms Lamp Oil ($1.85 per quart; $3.50 per half gallon). Other brands are available at comparable prices. If you use your lamps only during power failures and for an occasional lamplit dinner or social evening, $12 per gallon may not be an onerous price. But if oil is your sole source of light, you may find K-1 grade kerosene from a local gas station or fuel dealer a better long-term choice. In my neighborhood, K-1 is currently $1.65 a gallon. Make sure, however, that you do not get K-2 or, worse yet, No. 2 fuel oil. Not only do lower grade oils smoke and smell, they also gum up wicks and increase carbon deposits on them. In Aladdin lamps it is particularly important to use K-1 kerosene, Aladdin Lamp Oil ($3.75 per quart), or any other refined lamp oil to insure efficient operation. Also, do not use any scented oils in an Aladdin because they too can clog the wick.

A flat-wick lamp burns most efficiently—and safely—with a smoothly trimmed wick that produces a fan-shaped flame with no spikes of flame shooting out of it. The wick should not be visible above the slot in the burner. If it is, it will carbon up quickly, spew smoke, and cloud the chimney with soot. Using any oil lamp requires common sense and constant vigilance. Don't leave a burning lamp unattended. Don't place it on a wobbly table or near the edge of a table. Keep romping children, cats, and dogs at a distance.

A common and disastrous error is to forget how much heat is emitted from lamp chimneys, particularly from Aladdins, and to set them under a kitchen cabinet or hang them too close to a ceiling. The gap should be at least 30 inches. Then, too, Aladdins are extremely sensitive to changes in room temperature. A lamp that has been properly warmed up and then fine-tuned for optimum output can begin to smoke, blacken the mantle, and eventually shoot flames out of the chimney if the room temperature rises a few degrees—a frequent enough occurrence in a wood-heated room.

Buying Oil Lamps

Flat-wick lamps are readily available nationwide in a variety of outlets: gift shops, hardware, discount, department, and farm-supply stores. You will frequently find prices considerably below suggested retail. Lamplight Farms, 21125 Enterprise Avenue, Brookfield, Wisconsin 53005, 800-OIL LAMP, is primarily a wholesaler but is also happy to fill retail orders.

Better hardware and farm-supply stores carry Aladdin products. If you are unable to locate a dealer near you, write Aladdin Lamp Division, Dept. CJ, P.O. Box 100255, Nashville, Tennessee 37210, or call 800-456-1233.

Lehman Hardware and Appliances, Inc., P.O. Box 41, Kidron, Ohio 44636, 216-857-5441, which serves the Amish country of Ohio, has an extensive selection of non-electric lamps. Their prices on Aladdin lamps and Aladdin supplies—shipping and handling included—are significantly below suggested retail. Send $2 for Lehman's 84-page catalog.

THE GODDAM AUTOMOBILE

Getting a Grip on Ice and Snow

A guy who runs a service station and small tire business in my part of the woods tells me that tire chains are fast becoming obsolete. Why? Four-wheel drive—or at least front-wheel drive—in a wide variety of passenger vehicles for one thing. Radial tires for another. And mud and snow radials. And some chemical goo in all-weather tires that keeps them soft in the cold and so improves their traction. And there's all that salt that keeps roads ice-free and converts the underside of your car to rusty lacework. Last winter, my friend told me, he mounted hundreds of snow tires but only one set of chains.

Granted, recent years have brought improvements in both cars and tires that make them better able to cope with winter. But for all that, one crucial fact remains: When it comes to increasing your pulling power and decreasing your braking distance on ice and snow, chains leave even four-wheel drives and the best of snow tires dragging in the slush. The police in the western mountain areas know that and routinely close the roads to any vehicle not equipped with chains.

You don't have to be satisfied with either my word or that of the California Highway Patrol. The National Safety Council has done comparative tests on tires, snow tires, and chains and come up with some figures I'll cite to lend authority to my prejudices. A test with a front-wheel drive car on glare ice showed that snow tires gave 9 percent better pulling ability than a regular tire. The improvement with cable chains was 98 percent, with PL chains, 183 percent. In braking ability, the snow tire did 6 percent better than the regular tire; the cable chains, 33 percent; and the PL chains, 61 percent.

What are cable chains? What are PL chains? What's the difference between them, and how do they differ from still other types of chains, such as "P" and "RP"? When you buy chains, you will have to select one of these types, but before you can do that, you will have to consider two aspects of size: Not only must the chains fit your tires, but they must also be of the proper type to leave adequate clearance inside your wheel wells. The advent of compact and front-wheel drive vehicles has made this last point a critical one. So your first question isn't, "What kind of chains do I want?" but "What make and model car do I have, and what kind of chains can it take?"

The Society of Automotive Engineers has divided chains for use on passenger cars and light trucks into three size classes. SAE Class "S," which includes both PL chains and cable chains, is for vehicles with the most restricted wheel-well clearance and is the class needed for the majority of foreign and domestic passenger cars, whether front- or rear-wheel drive. SAE Class "U" fits a significant minority of passenger vehicles with larger clearance as well as pick-up trucks, big Broncos and Blazers, etc. SAE Class "W," which fits inside still larger wheel wells, the industry calls a "single truck, bus, and recreational vehicle" class. For larger trucks and buses and for tractors and other off-road equipment, clearance is no problem; and there are no classes. The owner's manual for your vehicle should tell you what class chains to use. If it doesn't, check with the dealer or manufacturer. Also, chain manufacturers publish charts in which you can look up your make and model of car, your tire size, and, therefore, the exact stock number of the chain you need.

Now, to return to types of chain itself: "PL" is an industry-wide designation for Class "S" passenger car chains with the low profile needed to fit inside wheel wells with small clearances. PL chains are also known as "1100 series" chains because they all carry stock numbers in the 1100s. Made of thinner steel and with less twist in longer cross links, PL chains do not stick up above the surface of the tire as much as heavier chains; and, if they are properly fitted—which is to say, snugly fitted—centrifugal force will not fling the cross chains away from the tire far enough that they will strike the wheel wells. Despite the fact that PL chains are made of comparatively light stock, the medium-carbon steel used in them makes them quite durable. Suggested retail prices for the common passenger-car sizes run from about $43 to $60.

PL chains are the only type of *chain* made specifically for vehicles with limited wheel-well clearance. However, the cable chain mentioned above is another Class "S" traction device that is legal in all states that may require the use of traction devices. Cable chain is just what the name suggests: Cable is used instead of chain, and traction is supplied by cylindrical lugs, which are strung like beads on the cable cross-members. The Security Chain Company of Portland, Oregon, pioneered cable chain, which now accounts for about 60 percent of Security's sales. Brian McCourt, Security's vice-president, listed the virtues that have made cable chain so popular in the western mountains. It is lighter and smaller and therefore easier to put on and take off than chain. These same qualities make it less noisy and bumpy if you have to drive on intermittent patches of bare pavement and also make it wear better under those same conditions. The trade-off for these benefits is a reduction of the grip that link chains provide for pulling and braking, but here too McCourt stresses that cable chains grip better on curves and in cornering and that they allow more controlled braking with front-wheel drives than the more aggressive link chains. Retail prices on Security cable chains in my local stores range from $35 to $50, depending on tire size.

If you drive a vehicle that will accommodate Class "U" chains and particularly if you do a lot of winter driving on unpaved and unsalted back roads, as I do, you will want heavier, more aggressive P ("Passenger Car") or RP ("Reinforced Passenger Car") chains (1200 and 1800 Series respectively). P chains are of heavier stock and have more twist than PL chains. In RP chains, both the bite and durability are increased even more by welding a small lug across the twisted link. My choice for backcountry driving in a light truck would be the Acco Weed reinforced V-bar chain, made by the American Chain Division of Acco Babcock. Suggested retail prices range from about $45 to $68. As with most things, of course, you may find all types of chains available at special sales for as little as half of suggested retail.

Putting Them On, Driving with Them, and Taking Them Off

The easiest way to put chains on is with a U-shaped wire gadget—the "applicator"—that slips onto your tire. For a rear-wheel-drive vehicle, lay the chain out behind the wheel. The lugs, if any, should face up, as should cross-chain hooks on PL chains. Gather the chain up behind the tire, slip the end links onto the hooks on the applicator, and drive the car forward for one full revolution of the wheel. The chain is now wrapped around the wheel with the applicator back to its original position, and you can hook the fasteners into the end links. Pick up the applicator instantly before you lose it in the snow. Drive for a quarter mile, and retighten the chains if necessary, making them as snug as you can get them by hand.

What forces you into chains is dangerous road conditions, and even with chains on, you should not drive over 30 mph. Not only is that a safe speed; it is also saving of your chains, which will wear out almost twice as fast if driven at 40 mph.

Once you're out of the snow, ice, slush, or mud, take your chains off. The friction, and resulting heat, from driving fast on dry pavement will damage your tires and chains. Most chain failures are due to abuse or improper mounting, not to flaws in the chain.

Major U.S. Manufacturers of Tire Chains

ACCO BABCOCK, INC.
American Chain Division
76 Acco Drive
P.O. Box 792
York, Pennsylvania 17405

CAMPBELL CHAIN
The Cooper Group
P.O. Box 728
Apex, North Carolina 27502

PEERLESS CHAIN COMPANY
1416 East 8th Street
P.O. Box 349
Winona, Minnesota 55987

SECURITY CHAIN COMPANY
621 S.E. Union
Portland, Oregon 97214

Utility Trailers for Highway, Field, and Woodlot

Choosing a trailer is a bit like choosing a horse. You have to know whether you want a pony for the kids to ride or a huge brute that can haul logs and plow fields. Once you're clear about that, you can start looking at individuals, peering into mouth, eye, and ear, checking out feet, legs, chest, and ankles, giving them a going over from nose to tail. And so it is with trailers, except that here the detailed examination proceeds from tongue to tail light.

The size of your trailer will be limited by the towing capacity of your vehicle. You may want to haul a cord of green mixed hardwood (about 5,000 pounds) or a yard of gravel (about 2,700 pounds), but your car may not want to at all. Your owner's manual will tell you the maximum Gross Trailer Weight (GTW) your car can handle. GTW is the total weight of the trailer itself plus its load. Automobile and RV dealers are continually amazed at how blithely their customers want to ignore and actually do ignore these weight limits. They'll tell you about the guy who wants to haul a 30-foot house trailer with a four-cylinder engine or about the other guy who already has a 30-foot house trailer and wonders why he keeps burning out transmissions in his compact car.

Few passenger cars are capable of hauling heavy trailers (4,000 pounds GTW and up). Some can handle medium trailers (up to 4,000 pounds), but most are happiest with light trailers (up to 2,000 pounds), and the lighter the better. The recommendation for my Toyota Tercel SR5 with manual transmission is 1,500 pounds. With an automatic transmission, it's a mere 700. And then some model cars don't want to have anything to do with trailers at all. The Chevrolet *RV/Trailering Guide* does not recommend the Sprint, Nova, Spectrum, or Corvette for trailer towing. The vehicles best suited to trailering are, not surprisingly, pickup trucks, four-wheel drives, and vans; but even vehicles rated for medium or heavy trailers should be ordered with special trailering features, which include a larger radiator, coolers for engine and transmission oil, and a trailer wiring harness.

Too heavy a trailer not only puts undue strain on your vehicle, inviting premature failure, but it is also quite literally a tail that can wag the dog and send it careening off the road or into oncoming traffic. For that reason, Federal Motor Carrier Safety Regulations require any trailer rated at 3,000 pounds GTW or above to have brakes on all axles. Car manufacturers' *recommendations* on brakes are even stricter, usually calling for brakes on any GTW exceeding 1,000 pounds; but in the real world I have yet to see a trailer under a 3,000 GTW that is equipped with brakes.

Weight capacity is the most important aspect of size to consider, but not the only one. Where you'll store the trailer and where you'll want to go with it will determine how wide and long you want it. My own trailer—a homemade job—has a bed size of 4-by-7 feet. Figure in the width of the wheels and fenders and the length of the tongue (the long metal shaft that connects the trailer to the hitch), and it's a little over 5 feet wide by 10 long. Winter storage space is at a premium around here, and when it's time to stow the trailer away in December, I'm glad it isn't any larger than it is. Also, I use it more off the road than on, often taking it into the woods on narrow dirt tracks to pick up firewood. Because it is only a couple of inches wider than my tractor, I can be reasonably sure that if the tractor fits between those two trees ahead of me, the trailer probably will, too. For people who do not go snaking their trailers around in tight places, a bed 5-by-8 feet is more practical, accommodating many items—such as 42-inch riding mowers—that a 4-foot wide bed will accept only with difficulty, if at all.

Let's assume, then, that you're in the market for a 5-by-8 trailer with a load capacity of 1,500 pounds. What are the specific features you're going to look for? Starting at the tip of the tongue, check the coupling. If the paint job isn't too heavy, you'll be able to read the specs stamped into the coupling and see that it's rated for at least 2,000 pounds. There should be a V-stand welded onto the bottom of the tongue to keep the coupling out of the mud when the trailer is not in use, also a handle on top to ease pushing the trailer around by hand. The safety chains (Class 1, 2,000 pounds; Class 2, 3,500) should be rugged enough for the GTW.

The tongue itself is a key component. That lesson was driven home to me a few years ago when some friends I was traveling with checked their trailer at a rest stop and found the tongue torn to within an inch of the breaking point. Very scary stuff. Look for 3-by-3-inch steel tubing ⅛-inch thick.

The ruggedest bed frames I have seen were in custom-built trailers made by a local fabricator in my neighborhood. They use channel iron on the perimeter rails (stuff shaped like a wide U with the open end of the U facing out) and square tubing ⅛-inch thick for the cross members. An 8-foot trailer should have four or five cross members under the bed. The more support under there, the better. Production-line trailers typically use 14-gauge tubing (a little over 1⁄16-inch thick) and heavy angle iron for bed frames. The side rails where the spring shackles tie into the bed should be either very heavy stuff or reinforced with tubing. If you want a tilting bed (one that you can raise at the front to dump a load), it should have a sturdy channel that fits down over the tongue and is held in place by heavy pins.

The two most common trailer bodies are the flat bed and the box-like metal body with a tailgate and with stake pockets all around so that you can add height with wooden sides. I prefer the second option. I can load gravel or sand to the trailer's capacity without having to raise the sides, and if I want to carry a light, bulky load (dry sawdust, hay, etc.), I have a firmer base to set my stakes into. Flat beds (some have low rails around them) are usually much cheaper, however.

If you'll use your trailer on rough terrain, wheels with larger diameters (12-, 13-, or 14-inch) will raise your axle over some of the rocks and stumps. If your priority is ease in loading a lawn tractor, tiller, or snowmobile, then you may well prefer 8-inch wheels. A DOT (Department of Transportation) stamp on the wheels assures you that they are an easily replaceable standard size.

The last—and often weakest—link between your load and the ground is your tires. Fortunately, you don't have to remember all that funny business about ply ratings and Load Range B, C, or D because the load capacity of each tire is marked on it in plain English. If your GTW is 1,850 pounds and the trailer has 5.30 × 12 tires in Load Range C, the handwriting on the sidewalls will reassure you that these tires, rated at 1,045 pounds each, will give you a combined load capacity of 2,090 pounds. (Load Range B, rated at 840 pounds in this tire size, would not do.)

Finally, if you're going to travel the highways, you need tail lights, brake lights, and turn signals. Any production-line trailer will have them. If you're building your own trailer or having one built, check details of type and placement in the Federal Motor Carrier Safety Regulations, available from your state motor vehicle division or state police. Unless your vehicle came with an adapter package, you will have to have an adapter installed so that you can plug the trailer lights into your vehicle. Some trailer dealers will install the adapter for you.

Finding the Right Trailer and the Right Hitch

Trailers are built by so many companies and with so many variations in components and details that you have to evaluate them practically trailer by trailer. Prices vary widely, too, trailers in the

4-by-6 to 5-by-8-foot class typically costing anywhere from about $500 to $1,200. The simple flatbeds are cheaper, regardless of bed size; metal sides and tailgates drive the price up. Rather than recommend specific trailers by model and name here, I would instead suggest the following buying strategy: Go out and look at a lot of trailers in the weight and size class you want. Comparing several brands out on the lots will give you a much clearer idea of the difference between a solidly built, heavy-duty trailer and the lighter models. After you've done enough sifting, you may be able to go back to one of the production-line trailers you've seen, feeling sure that it is indeed the one you want. If not, search out a reliable welder and fabricator with some experience in trailer building. Then you can sit down with him and his part supplier's catalog and specify not only which axle, springs, wheels, and tires you want but also special dimensions and features that fit your particular needs. If you know exactly what you want and if you know a welder who can give it to you, you'll probably be happiest with a custom-made job that will not cost you much more, if any more, than a production-line trailer.

The two major U.S. manufacturers of trailer hitches are Draw-Tite, 40500 Van Born Road, Canton, Michigan 48188, and Reese Products, P.O. Box 1706, Elkhart, Indiana 46515. Class I hitches, usually bumper mounted, are for trailers up to 2,000 pounds GTW. Class II hitches, which bolt to the tow vehicle frame, are heavier and handle trailers between 2,000 and 3,500 pounds GTW. Your owner's manual may well recommend a specific make and model hitch for your car. If not, check with your car dealer or RV dealer. By far the most knowledgeable people I found on the subject of trailer hitches and general trailer outfitting were at my local RV dealership.

Cartop Racks

If you drive a compact car but do not live a compact life—and I don't know anyone who can manage to live a compact life in the country—you will need a cartop rack. In fact, you'll probably need one no matter what kind of car you drive. Country life, almost by definition, sticks out at the ends, hangs over the edges, refuses to be contained; and at some point, you will exceed the limits of even an outsized passenger car. You'll want to take home some 14-foot 2-by-10s from the lumber yard or transport your johnboat to your favorite pickerel pond. You don't need a truck or trailer, but you do need some extra carrying capacity. Enter the roof rack.

There are more cartop gadgets out there than you can shake a ski pole at. I have a list of twenty-five manufacturers, foreign and domestic, in front of me right now; and the number of different models, accessories, adapters, and what-not must approach a small million. So I'm going to be ruthless about this and say that any halfway serious country hauler can eliminate certain categories right away.

The first things you can forget about are the "soft" racks. These are not racks at all but configurations of foam or rubber pads strung onto webbing which is in turn hooked into a car's rain gutters or door recesses and stretched tight across the roof. Some of them are rigged with ski holders, and in this same category I include the slotted, closed-cell foam blocks used for car-topping small boats. None of these rigs can handle heavy loads, and I simply don't believe in the reliability of any strap systems.

Next, I would avoid "dedicated" racks, that is, racks that can carry one item and one item only. Ski racks are the most plentiful of the dedicated racks, and if you'll never ever carry anything but skis, well and good. But if you garden, pick up an occasional piece of furniture at a lawn sale, do a little building, and go fishing as well as ski—if, in short, you live a country life—you need something much more versatile than a ski rack.

That narrows the field down to the "hard" multipurpose rack, and within this category your choice of a cheap, homemade rack, an expensive and sophisticated one, or something in between will depend on your specific needs and your specific vehicle. For example: I have a 1971 Chevrolet Blazer whose main mission in life is to carry me, a few passengers, and one or more canoes to rivers I like. My rack is a couple of 2-by-4s padded with old carpeting and bolted to the roof. If, however, I had a new BMW (fat chance!) and wanted to haul $2,000-worth of racing bikes around all summer and a comparably expensive load of skis all winter, I would be reluctant to drill holes in the roof and tie my cargo down with some nylon rope. Instead, I would buy one of the carefully engineered and well-built multipurpose racks that offer a wide selection of accessories designed for carrying special equipment.

The questions you need to ask, then, to sort out the many choices open to you among hard, nondedicated racks are these: How heavy are the loads you want to carry? Do you need a rack readily adaptable to different kinds of loads? Is the rack you're considering easy to put on and take off the car? Is it made of materials that resist rust and corrosion? Can you lock the rack onto the car and your cargo onto the rack? Does the rack fit your car? That's a key question indeed, and subquestions to it are: (1) Will it fit both or all your cars if you have more than one? And (2) can it be adapted to fit a new car? Finally, how much do you want to spend? Let's look at four options in the light of these questions.

My 2-by-4s, with their huge bearing surface, are great load carriers. Two canoes (about 160 pounds) are duck soup, and for a limited run, I wouldn't hesitate to put on three (or about 250 pounds). With enough rope and time, I can hitch just about anything to this rack; but adaptation to loads other than canoes, lumber, or other large, simple items is not fast and easy. This rack is obviously a permanent installation. I pay a penalty in lowered gas mileage caused by the increased wind resistance (I've seen estimates of 5 percent or more for an unloaded rack), but because I drive this vehicle very rarely without a load, that is no great concern to me. Weather resistance is superb; there's nothing to rust. No locks of any kind, but then nobody wants my 2-by-4s, and I don't leave my canoe parked overnight in downtown Philadelphia. The fit is as secure as the roof itself. Because the roof of this ancient Blazer lacks rain gutters or anything else you could hook a rack to, you have to mount a permanent rack on it or mount brackets to which you can clamp a removable rack. In short, for an investment of a little time and less than $5, I have a rack that suits my needs and vehicle admirably.

The Quik-N-Easy Universal Car Top Carrier (Quik-N-Easy Products, Inc., 934 West Foothill Boulevard, P.O. Box 878, Monrovia, California 91016, 818-358-0562) gives you a rugged rack with some conveniences the bolted-down 2-by-4s can't deliver. Quik-N-Easy's basic kit is four cast-aluminum stanchions (suggested retail about $30) which clamp onto rain gutters and to which you can bolt two 2-by-4s. The aluminum doesn't rust. Cam levers on the clamps make mounting and removal very quick and easy indeed. Rigged with 2-by-4s, this system cannot, of course, be easily mounted on a different car. However, for $20 more, you can get two round metal crossbars and the four yokes needed to attach them to the stanchions. This setup is easily adjusted to different widths. The Quik-N-Easy is an excellent basic rack at a reasonable price. Its use is limited, however, to cars with rain gutters.

The poorest of the rigid racks are the low-priced affairs you're likely to find at discount stores, some auto-supply stores, and in the catalogues of the big mail-order houses. My local discount store, for example, sells a Raco Jumbo Load 60″ Bar Carrier for $24.99. The crossbar is a light-gauge stamped steel. Because the bar is open at the bottom, this rack wails like a banshee when you get rolling along at highway speeds. The open bottom in the bars lets the rubber-padded feet on which the rack rests slide back and forth to adjust for car width. Adjustment requires a wrench and is both irksome and time-consuming. The rack is secured to the car by means of inadequately padded gutter hooks that scratch the car finish and have to be tightened with a wrench. Because the attachment bolts and nuts are not rustproof, they can (and do) corrode into immobility and make the rack next to impossible to remove. At best, mounting and removal are such a nuisance that you're likely to leave the rack on the car and so boost your fuel consumption significantly. The black paint on the crossbar and stanchions quickly rubs off and leaves those parts susceptible to rust, too. Under a heavy load or excessive tightening down, the supporting feet can dent the car roof. If you use a rack only rarely, you may feel that this rack's low price compensates for its inconvenience and poor quality. The only use I can happily imagine for this rack and others of its ilk is none at all.

At the opposite end of the scale are the carefully engineered and well-made multipurpose racks of which Thule and Yakima are among the front runners. They are, it seems to me, the only rational route to go if neither the bolted-on 2-by-4s or the Quik-N-Easy will meet your needs. Depending on your car and the rack model you want, you can pay anywhere from about $55 to $115 for the basic four stanchions and crossbars, pricey but worth it. What you get is a rack that fits your car precisely, will let you carry heavy loads safely—Thule's maximum recommended load is 165 pounds; Yakima's is 200—and will not damage your car. The high-quality rack companies have done an excellent job of devising clamp and stanchion systems to fit gutterless cars. The feet that rest on the roof are designed to bear on the very edges of the roof, where the roof is strongest. However, the configuration I personally much prefer for a detachable rack is one that mounts in rain gutters, and if I knew I was going to do a lot of car-topping of everything from a couple of pairs of skis to a few bags of cement, one factor that would determine my choice of a car would be whether it had solid rain gutters formed by two layers of metal (roof and side of car) stamped to fit together and then welded. Some modern cars have rain gutters that in fact deflect rain and are decorative but will not hold up under a heavily loaded rack. Hook the fingers of both your hands into them and hang your full weight on them. If they give, you may not be able to use a rack designed for use with rain gutters. And in any case, consult the detailed charts that rack manufacturers have to tell you which racks will fit your car.

The other benefit, aside from perfect fit, that the good multipurpose racks give you is a wide choice of attachments custom designed for transporting equipment like bikes, sailboards, skis, and kayaks. These accessories don't come cheap. A Thule lockable vertical ski rack for three pairs of skis, for example, retails for $60, a kayak carrier for $48. How often you travel with such items and how expensive they are themselves will determine what, if any, accessories you may want to buy. Ease of mounting and removal of these racks is exemplary. Large knobs (available with locks) tighten the clamps onto the car. Adjustment to another car is equally simple, provided the other car takes the same model stanchion. Weatherproofing is excellent. For its stanchions, Yakima uses Zytel, a space-age nylon composite as strong as steel; fittings are stainless steel; crossbars are polyethylene coated steel. Every component in the Thule system is either of rustproof material (e.g., aluminum) or doubly rustproofed. The crossbar, for example, is first galvanized, then polymer coated.

Most of the more expensive, multipurpose rack systems offer locks that lock the rack to the car, others that lock equipment to the rack. A determined and skillful thief with the right tools can crack any of them, but there is also no doubt that rack locks will deter the amateur who might be tempted to lift an unprotected pair of skis or twist those easy-off knobs and heist a nice looking rack.

Some Manufacturers of Multipurpose Roof Racks

AUTOMAXI
3065 North Rockwell
Chicago, Illinois 60618
312-588-7634

BARRECRAFTERS
P.O. Box 158
Shelburne, Vermont 05482
802-985-3321

BIC SPORT USA
1021 Sherman Avenue
Hamden, Connecticut 06514
203-281-7877

TERZO
1860 Acacia Avenue
Compton, California 90220
213-603-9911

THULE
One Westchester Plaza
Elmsford, New York 10523
914-592-4812

YAKIMA
P.O. Drawer 4899
Arcata, California 95521
707-822-2908

YARD AND GARDEN, FIELD AND FOREST

For the Birds

Ignorance is rarely bliss, but you can luck out. Some ten years ago a friend gave Rita and me a bird feeder. It consisted of two wooden bowls (reject salad bowls from a turning mill) mounted on a dowel so that the small bowl served as a seed holder, the large one as a roof and squirrel baffle. We hung the feeder on the back porch, and come October, we bought a 50-pound bag of sunflower seed. We also hung up an old onion bag full of suet I stripped from the innards of lambs who had gone to slaughter. Capital outlay: zero. Operating expenses: about $15 per annum for seed.

Our good luck would have it that birds start locating their winter food sources quite early in the fall (October, even September in severe climes), and we had had native wit enough to know we should put the feeder on the south side of the house where it would get the sun and not be tossed about by the icy blasts of the northwest wind. A nearby lilac bush provided a roost where birds could line up and wait their turn at the feeder. With this simple setup we have attracted chickadees, evening grosbeaks, purple finches, juncos, redpolls, house and song sparrows, blue jays, nuthatches, hairy and downy woodpeckers, and gray squirrels, to name only the more frequent guests.

In the meantime, having consulted a number of books and spoken with a few experts on attracting birds, I find that my wife and I did nothing drastically wrong but that with a little more knowledge and very little more expense we might have drawn more species to our dooryard.

In our choice of feed, we were right to offer sunflower seeds alone rather than a commercial birdseed mix. Most mixes contain a number of ingredients—wheat, milo, red millet, hulled oats, and rice—that birds do not like and therefore discard. It is far more efficient and economical to buy and offer the preferred foods—sunflower seeds, cracked corn, white proso millet, niger (or thistle), and suet—separately. All the expert birders agree that sunflower seed is an excellent food; some, however, think the oil (black) sunflower is more attractive to birds than the black-striped sunflower; others feel there is no difference. The difference in cost is minimal. Prices per 50 pounds of seed at my local Agway store are: black-striped sunflower $13.99; oil sunflower $14.99. In some areas, the black-striped may be cheaper. In any case, the moral is simple: Either variety will do very nicely, and if you feel inclined to experiment, try both kinds and become your own expert. Twenty-five pounds of white millet cost $7.50 and the same amount of cracked corn, $4.85. The most expensive seed is niger, which I priced at between $.99 and $1.19 per pound. By far the best prices will be found at your local grain and feed store, not at specialty birding shops and mail-order houses or at grocery stores.

The reasons for offering these staples separately have to do with gravity, birds' feeding habits, and controlling access to the feed. Because some birds, like sparrows and mourning doves, feed primarily on the ground, that's the place to put the white millet and cracked corn they prefer. The primary sources of food for other species are seeds and insects found in trees, but whatever is up in the air may well fall down. Hence, these birds will go anywhere the food is. The only argument against feeding all the birds on the ground is that many of the smaller species you most want to attract get shouldered aside by squirrels, blue jays, and other larger birds.

The solution is to scatter ground feed at a couple of sites and place elevated feeders at others. One of the best feeder designs for offering sunflower seeds to small birds is the tube feeder. This feeder operates on the hopper principle, and the multiple feeding ports allow several birds to feed at once without squabbling. A hanging tube feeder discourages ground-feeding birds, and it can be made even more selective by removing the perches. Without perches, the feeder is accessible mainly to small birds, like chickadees, titmice, and finches that can both cling to and feed from the ports. The same feeder with the perches left in it will draw larger perching birds, such as evening grosbeaks.

Droll Yankees' 16-inch Yankee Feeder, which a wildlife biologist I spoke with called "the Cadillac of bird feeders," sells for $21.50; the 21-inch Superfeeder for $37.50. (Droll Yankees' bird feeders are available at some hardware stores and gift shops, through Duncraft and Audubon mail-order catalogs, or by writing Droll Yankees, P.O. Box 98, Foster, Rhode Island 02825). An Oldsmobile of bird feeders in a store near me went for $16.95. Very serviceable Fords and Chevvies of a thick, durable plastic can be had from $10 to $12. They lack the metal trim that the more expensive models have around the feeding ports to prevent squirrels from gnawing at the holes and enlarging them—not a major problem if you can keep your squirrels baffled or busy elsewhere. Tube feeders meant for the tiny niger seed, which is much favored by goldfinches and the northern finches, have much smaller feeding ports and are available in similar price ranges.

The tube feeder has great practical advantages. It is the most weatherproof of feeders; it keeps the birds and their feces out of the feed, which means less cleaning for you and less chance of spreading disease among the birds; and its slender shape makes it minimally susceptible to the wind.

Heavy plastic versions of my two salad bowls have the advantages of being easy to wipe clean and offering a slipperier baffle for the squirrels to slide off. Their large surface area does make them windcatchers, however, and they are best hung in well-sheltered locations. Some models (Seed Saver, 10-inch diameter dome,

$17.50; Big Top, 15-inch diameter dome, $37.50, both from Duncraft, Penacook, New Hampshire 03303) have adjustable domes that let you narrow the feed opening for small birds or open it wide to invite the whole world in. My Agway store carries a 14-inch, nonadjustable model for $14.95.

Suet is an energy-rich food that woodpeckers and nuthatches are particularly fond of but that many other species also eat. If you want something more substantial than an onion bag for a feeder, you can buy suet feeders made of rubber-coated wire for $5 to $8 (the rubber coating precludes the unlikely possibility of a bird's eye or tongue freezing to supercooled metal).

I suppose the greatest measure of our ignorance was that we did not consider squirrels pests but took great pleasure in their acrobatic efforts to get at our feeder. That's a bit of blissful ignorance I'll persist in, but what would I do if they got out of hand? Alan Pistorius recommends strewing more ground feed to distract them. He also warms up on cold winter mornings by pitching tennis balls at the more importunate ones. So when you're laying in your bird seed, you may want to pick up a few tennis balls, too (three practice balls for $1.95 at sporting goods stores everywhere).

Reading, Etc.

The Audubon Society Guide to Attracting Birds by Stephen W. Kress (Charles Scribner's Sons, New York, 1985, $24.95) stresses that while feeding birds may be fun for you, the very best thing you can do for the birds is provide year-round habitat for them, and Kress offers landscaping and planting strategies appropriate for every region in the United States.

For solid information, common sense, enjoyable reading, and entertaining insights into birders and birding, pick *The Country Journal Book of Birding and Bird Attracting* by Alan Pistorius (W. W. Norton and Co., New York, 1981, $15.95).

A thorough and thoroughly reliable book highly respected by

ornithologists is John K. Terres, *Songbirds in Your Garden* (3d ed., Hawthorne Books, Inc., New York, 1977, paperback $5.95).

National Audubon's booklet *Banquet for Birds* is an excellent short treatment of bird feeding. It's available from The National Audubon Society, Information Services, 950 Third Avenue, New York, New York 10022, for $2.

Debugging Yourself

Poets have always been enthusiastic about the darling buds and flowery meads of May, but there's little talk of the noisome bugs that breed so profusely at this time of year, making sheer hell out of evening hours in the garden or on your favorite trout stream. When it comes to fending off the bugs, I resort to three stratagems: voodoo, protective clothing, and insect repellents, in that order. My assumption is that the minimal means needed to accomplish a task properly is the appropriate means.

The density of the bug attack and personal sensitivity to insect bites will, of course, determine who reaches for what remedy when. If black fly bites make you swell up like a green and yellow balloon, you'll resort to repellents long before the person in whom black flies leave only a small bloody hole. But despite these personal differences, the principle of moving from the lesser to the greater defense as needed remains valid.

Voodoo is the cheapest form of bug defense, and it shouldn't be written off as useless simply because it doesn't cost anything. Perhaps it will sound more respectable if I call it a psychogenerated immunity or, if you will, a mental thick skin. But whatever the name, a cultivated indifference to bugs is a reality that cannot be explained by physical factors alone. Why is it that the same cloud of black flies that has one man screaming and waving his arms frantically leaves his partner in the canoe unperturbed? Bugs do like some people more than others, but in this particular case, the serene chap has as many of them buzzing about his ears as the frantic fellow does. Chances are that the individual who is less disturbed by the bugs has a history of long exposure to them and has developed greater tolerance for them. So when my fishing partners say, "Aren't these jeezly bugs driving you out of your wig?" I smile cheerfully and say, "What bugs?"

But even for folks who are hardened to the local variety of pest, a time comes when voodoo no longer works. The aerial assault is enough to make Buddha squirm. At this point you resort to protective clothing or insect repellent or a combination of the two. Because I have yet to find an insect repellent, either natural or synthetic, that I really *like* to put on, I try locking the bugs out first.

If you're up against black flies, you have to close up even the tiniest gaps into which they might crawl. I use big rubber bands cut out of an old inner tube to snug my pant cuffs tight around my boots. A shirt that buttons down the front and at the cuffs offers far too many gaps for comfort. Velro strips sewn into the cuff slits let you seal off that access route; but if the bugs are really thick, you'll need a long-sleeved, snug-fitting cotton turtleneck to eliminate the gaps down your front. A lightweight long-sleeved polypropylene underwear shirt is good, too; but the turtleneck has the added advantage of giving you unbroken armor from your waist to right up under your ears. Also, if you're using a headnet, you can snug it down over the turtleneck to make an (almost) bugproof joint.

The headnet I've liked best has a solid cloth top and two stiff hoops that hold the net (and therefore the bugs) away from your face. An elasticized drawstring at the bottom lets you close it up tight around your neck. The net I have must have been made for the French Foreign Legion. A stamp in the top of it says "Armee,

1954—J. Miller Cie., Villeurbanne," and how I got hold of it I could not venture to guess. But the model is not exotic or unavailable. I've seen a similar net in the Campmor catalogue for $4.99 (Campmor, P.O. Box 997, Paramus, New Jersey 07653-0997).

Headnets minus the hoops will do the job too, provided you have a hat that is broad-brimmed and stiff enough to keep the net away from your face. If the net has no drawstring at the bottom, it should be plenty long enough to tuck way down into your collar. Also, if you're in no-see-um country, you'll need a netting that is fine enough to foil those tiny little creatures as well as the larger black flies and mosquitoes. And with netting that fine, you may soon be driven to ask which fate you prefer: suffocation inside the net or being eaten alive without it.

A silk balaclava (about $5 from most outfitters) or one you can fashion at home out of a T-shirt is another form of head protection that keeps the bugs out of your ears, nose, mouth, and hair while leaving your vision unimpaired, though some flies will manage to sneak in around the edges of the eye opening in the balaclava.

To complete your antibug outfit, add a pair of cheap cotton work gloves (about $2) or polypropylene gloves ($7 to $12) with snug wristlets that will form a tight, overlapping joint with your shirt. If shirtsleeve and glove keep pulling apart, sew a long elasticized wristlet onto the gloves.

If all this sounds something like a suit of armor, that's just what it is; and in mosquito country the armor should be thick enough and loose fitting enough that the mosquitoes can't probe through your shirt with those long proboscises of theirs. A thin, sweaty cotton shirt or tightly stretched chinos are no barrier at all to a hungry mosquito.

On the subject of armor, this is the place to mention bug suits, which are made of a polyester, nylon, and cotton mesh and then treated with DEET insect repellent. These suits look like a wispy version of chain mail and have the advantage of encasing you in a layer of repellent while keeping it off your skin. Many canoeists who travel in northern Canada, where the black flies and mosquitoes are so thick they can literally endanger health and sanity, report that bug jackets are the greatest invention since flapjacks. Ben's Bug Armor is available through L. L. Bean, other sporting goods stores, or directly from Mowatt Sporting Goods, P.O. Box 158, Brewer, Maine 04412, 800-USA-BENS. The jacket and pants retail for $29.95 each. The Shoo-Bug jacket ($27.95) and pants ($23.95) are also available through sporting goods stores, some mail-order houses, and from the manufacturer, Cole Products of America, P.O. Box 81336, Lincoln, Nebraska 68501-1336.

Baby Oil, Citronella, and DEET

The human mind keeps breeding ways to defeat bugs almost as prolifically as a swamp breeds mosquitoes. One black-fly trap that some gardeners swear by is a swath of aluminum foil wrapped around a hat, bright side out, and soaked with baby oil. The flies are drawn to this contraption and then bog down in the oil. Another product that would seem completely unlikely as an insect repellent but that works for many people is Avon's Skin-So-Soft, $5.49 for 8 ounces from your local Avon lady.

Oil of citronella is a key ingredient in almost all of the traditional woodsman's potions, and if you would like to experiment with concoctions of your own, volume one of Horace Kephart's venerable *Camping and Woodcraft* (New York: Macmillan Publishing Company, Inc., first published in 1917) contains a number of recipes on pages 243–249. A recipe favored in my circle of Maine woods travelers calls for 2 parts baby oil, 1 part Vaseline, 1 part citronella, 1 part camphor, and (optional) 1/4 part pine tar. Heat all the ingredients together until they are warm enough to blend thoroughly, then pour into small bottles. If you don't want to mix your own, there are commercial repellents ready-made from natural oils, such as Double Strength Green Ban ($5.50 for 2½ fluid ounces), an Australian product available nationwide at sporting goods and backpacking stores, and Royal Guard Bug-A-Way (about $2.25 for 2 fluid ounces).

Of the synthetics on the market, DEET (N-N-diethyl-mtoluamide) is the active ingredient that has proved more long-lasting and more effective against a broad spectrum of insects than ethyl hexanediol or any of the other active ingredients used in small percentages in some repellents. Repellents that are 100 percent DEET, such as Ben's 100, Muskol, Repel 100, and Old Time Woodsman's Jungle Plus, are now the repellents of choice in areas of heavy insect infestation. But DEET is a potent compound, and like many other beneficial substances (such as aspirin and bourbon), it should be used with care and moderation. It is readily absorbed into the system through the skin, and isolated cases of toxic and allergic reactions to it have been reported. Children's small body volume makes them even more prone to adverse reactions. Be particularly sparing in your use of 100 percent DEET with children, and avoid prolonged exposure even to those repellents with lower percentages of DEET (for example, Old Time Woodsman, 27 percent, Cutter Cream, 33 percent, and Off!, 15 percent).

To DEET or not to DEET? My own response is that I will if I'm in a state of utter desperation, but I won't if I'm not. I carry both a repellent made of natural oils and a bottle of Ben's 100. If voodoo and protective clothing are not enough, I reach first for the citronella, then, only as a last resort, for the DEET. The very bottom line is that any insect repellent should be used with caution.

Of the forms in which repellents come, the liquids in squeeze bottles are far and away the most efficient and economical. Aerosols should be avoided for environmental reasons. Prices may vary considerably, depending on where and in what quantities you buy. A 1¼-ounce bottle of Ben's 100 costs $2.39 at my local drugstore. Two ounces of Muskol goes for about $6.

Moving Snow by Hand

Mechanized snow removal works on one of two principles. You either push the snow out of your way (snow plow), or you pick it up here and put it down there (bucket loader). A variation on Principle 2 is the snowthrower, which gobbles it up here and throws it over there. Manual snow removal works on the same two principles, with you instead of a truck, tractor, or Briggs and Stratton engine supplying the energy.

Even if you are blessed (or cursed) with some kind of snow-moving machinery, you'll still need some hand tools, if for no other reason than to dig a path to the barn or garage to start the tractor. Shovels and scoops also do the innumerable little jobs for which using a tractor and snow plow would be like hitting a tack with a sledge hammer: clearing drifts away from the woodshed or back steps, opening a path from kitchen to chicken coop to sheep shed, digging a guest's car out of a snowbank.

For shoveling snow, about the worst possible tool you can buy is a snow shovel, and tool manufacturers would do the public a great service if they discontinued this line altogether. The tool labeled "snow shovel" in your local hardware store and in the catalogs has a wide rectangular blade (usually about 15-by-18 inches) which is simply a flat hunk of steel, aluminum, or plastic stamped or molded into a slightly curved shape. Because it is difficult to attach a handle to a large metal or plastic waffle, the tool is either structurally weak or, if reinforced, structurally messy. Because the blade is virtually sideless, light powder snow dribbles off, and blocks of heavy, wet snow slide off it if the tool is not held level. Shoveling snow is hard enough work without making a balancing act of it as well.

Far superior to snow shovels are the various tools that go by such names as "grain scoop," "sand and gravel scoop," "barn and snow shovel," "coal and street shovel," etc. For powdery, cold-weather snow, the grain scoop is the ideal tool. Because a grain scoop's purpose in life is to move large amounts of light materials quickly, it has a huge, high-backed, high-sided blade. Steel would make these outsized blades inordinately heavy, so grain scoops are made of aluminum or plastic. Typical weights for aluminum scoops run between 4 and 5 pounds. Plastic ones are lighter by a pound or so.

Scoop handles have D-grips and are usually 26 to 30 inches long. D-grip handles as long as 40 inches can be had, however, and if you're tall, you may well be more comfortable with a longer handle. Although you will find some "general purpose scoops" with the long, straight shovel handle (usually about 50 inches long), these are a poor choice. For moving snow, you don't need the leverage of a long handle, but you do need the control the D-grip gives you. The other thing to look for is adequate "handle lift." Handle lift is the angle the handle forms with the ground if you lay the blade flat on the ground. A snow shoveler wants quite a steep angle of lift so that he or she will not have to bend way down to pick up a load. By contrast, a coal miner lying on his belly in a 36-inch seam wants a shovel with practically no handle lift at all.

Aluminum scoops can't take rough usage. You can't chop ice with them or whang them into rocks. Nor will they survive the cutting and prying process required for moving heavy, packed snow. The first aluminum grain scoop I owned I literally tore in half by asking things of it that it was not designed to do. Scoops, whether aluminum or plastic, are for scooping, and that's that.

For rougher tasks you need a steel shovel. The one that has served me well for years has a flat blade, a square point, and sides that angle up to keep the snow in. The blade measures 11-by-13½ inches; the D-grip handle is 32 inches long and has 21 inches of lift (measured at the end of the D-grip). The tool weighs 5 pounds and fits neatly into the well of a VW Rabbit. This is the one I use when the town plow has rolled a hard-packed heap of spring snow up against my garage doors. It will take the guff of slicing and levering out heavy blocks of snow, and you can use it to chop up those clumps of almost ice that keep the doors from opening. If the edge starts to curl from too much whacking, you can reshape it with a hammer and file.

Among the snow-pushing tools, I've found little use on a country place for the baby snow plows (18 to 24 inches wide by 10 or 11 inches high) that are mounted on long handles and called, logically enough, "snow pushers." They may have their uses on smooth surfaces, like porch decks or sidewalks, but since I have no sidewalks and only a small porch, I don't own a snow pusher.

The pushing tool I would not be without, however, is the Garant Galvanized Sleigh Shovel. This is essentially a wide galvanized pan with raised sides and a tubular-steel handle. Wooden and plastic models are available, too, but because the wooden ones have runners on the bottom and the plastic ones abrade easily and are grooved to add rigidity, I much prefer the galvanized models which slide easily in any direction and are more durable. You push the scoop ahead of you, "mowing" a swath through the snow. When the pan is full, you turn it to the side, dump your load, then proceed as before. The flat bottom of the scoop lets you clean right down to the ground, yet it slides over rocks, lumps, and bumps without hanging up. The depth and density of the snow and your own strength and endurance will dictate how much you rely on this tool. If the snow is fluffy and not too deep, you can mow a surprisingly long swath before you have to dump; and I frequently use the sleigh shovel to clear my driveway of light snowfalls. In late winter the tool is ideal for sliding under heavy mounds of packed snow and sledding them off out of your way. The sleigh shovel's great virtue is that you don't have to lift anything and you can transport heavy loads short distances with a minimum of effort.

Finally, don't forget that the sleigh shovel is indeed a *sleigh* shovel: Small children love to sit in it and enlist a willing adult to push, pull, and crack the whip with them on the skim snow of a frozen dooryard. It beats shoveling snow any day.

Prices, Quality, Dimensions

The solid socket construction used in better grade garden forks, spades, and shovels, which have to stand up under great strain, would be a needless expense in tools used for scooping and moving loose materials. The scoops and shovels discussed here are therefore all of "hollow-backed" or "open back" construction; and the better quality tools differ not in construction but only in the weight and type of materials used.

With their scoops and shovels appropriate for snow moving, the three major American tool manufacturers follow the same good, better, and best grading system they use with all their tools and stamp the grade designations on the tool handles. True Temper's grades are, from top to bottom, Professional, Premium, and Quality, and each grade is further identified by five, four, or three stars. Union Fork and Hoe's grades are Union Deluxe, Union Standard, and Union. In Ames aluminum scoops, the top line is called Ames; and the next notch down is Ram. In the steel shovels Red Edge—Three Star is tops; Knoxall, next. Anything called "Promotional" in anybody's line is the lowest grade. If your local stores carry other makes, find out what the grading system is.

The most common blade sizes in aluminum grain scoops are the No. 10 (14¾-by-18 inches), No. 12 (15¼-by-19 inches), and No. 14 (15¾-by-20 inches). The differences look miniscule on paper, but the tools in hand feel very different indeed. So pick the one that hefts best for you. The list price for True Temper's top quality No.

10 scoop is $40.59; for the Premium grade of the same size it's $26.49. The prices for an Ames and a Ram in the same sizes are $38.70 and $29.90. What you're getting for those extra 10 or 15 dollars is a heavier gauge aluminum and a higher grade ash in the handle. These are light tools for a light job, and I personally lean toward the lighter, cheaper tool as long as it is well made. Is the head fitted smoothly to the handle? Are there any projecting corners or edges that will nick your hands? Are rivets driven squarely through the handle? If the D-grip is a one-piece plastic type, is it guaranteed against cracking and breaking? Is it comfortable to hold, and firmly attached? If it is wood and metal, is the cob (crosspiece) locked in place so that it will not work loose? Is the handle itself straight-grained and with the oval "flowers" turned to the sides of the tool?

In steel, Ames Street or Snow Shovel with the D-handle is just about the twin of my vintage steel shovel: 11-by-13½-inch blade, 34-inch D-grip handle, about 5½ pounds, and a list price of $14.20. So is True Temper's Barn and Snow Shovel, with almost identical specs and for only 49 cents more.

Garant Galvanized Sleigh Shovels are sold by the Garant Corporation, P.O. Box 5156, Manchester, New Hampshire, and can be had in 16-, 20-, 24-, and 28-inch widths for $19.80, $28.60, $30.30, and $32.30 respectively. I prefer the 28-inch one, which handles a lot of snow and two small children.

Tools for Taming the Wild Side

Though a gardener's main mission may be helping desirable plants grow up, he or she inevitably spends some time knocking undesirable ones down. There are many knocking-down tools available, but before I discuss the ones I like, I should say there are some I dislike vehemently. They go by such names as "weed cutter" or "grass whip" and consist of a serrated, double-edged blade mounted on a stick either in an L shape or with a D-shaped hoop. They are swung like a golf club, and if they meet much resistance in dense grass, they will come up short and merely squash the grass flat. Their round handles tend to twist in the hands, and it takes a lot of energy just to keep the tool lined up properly. After half an hour with one of these hacking tools, you're likely to find yourself flat on the ground, not the grass and weeds you're attacking.

The better hand tools for cutting grass, weeds, and light brush have, by contrast, curved, razor-sharp blades that both hack and slice. Which capacity of the tool you choose to emphasize will depend on the density and toughness of the greenery to be cut.

For light trimming around yard and garden, a sickle may be all you will ever need. With a practiced hand, you can trim within millimeters of rocks, steps, and house foundations and dispense (almost) with grass shears. Shears remain a necessary evil for trimming off those few wisps that hug the rocks too snugly for your sickle to reach them, but for any real cutting, grass shears are an abomination. In the typical vertical-squeeze, horizontal-cut model, your fingers have to provide the power not only to cut the grass but also to activate *two* hinges and buck a spring, an absurdly complex power train for such a simple task. Sheep shears have only one hinge, but with them, too, most of your energy goes into fighting the spring hinge rather than cutting grass. And if the shears are held parallel to the ground, as they must be to trim grass, the hand is forced into an awkward, tiring position.

There is also, of course, the motor-driven option, one of those gadgets that decapitates grass blades with a rapidly whirling snippet of nylon cord. These machines offend my sense of proportion. They require much too high an expenditure both in dollars and in the earth's resources to do a job that a simple curved blade accomplishes very neatly.

I hold the sickle loosely and practically throw it at my target with a quick flick of the wrist. This means that you need a round, contoured handle that can be held in a relaxed grip without flying out of the hand. I often hook my index finger over the shoulder of the handle for added security. The whole tool should be balanced around the axis of the handle so that the tip of the blade tends neither to float up into the air nor to nose-dive into the ground. A sickle should be light enough that fifteen minutes of use does not leave you with a lame wrist yet heavy enough that the weight of the tool helps carry it through grass and weeds. For me that means 10 ounces, with the weight forward in the blade, not in the handle. To check the weight and balance of a sickle, pick it up, use it. If it feels right, it is right.

When it comes to shape, I prefer an open to a tight curve in the blade because I find it easier to cut close to my many rocks with the open blade. But whether open or tight, the sickle blade both slices and hacks; and if you find you are biting off more than the blade and your wrist can chew, simply take a narrower cut, which reduces what you have to cut through and favors the slicing action of the tip of the blade rather than the hacking action at the back of the curve.

My favorite sickle is an ancient, hammered-steel affair that has a decidedly open blade. I doubt its like can be found anywhere short of the village smithy, and I am not aware of a single sickle on the market that I could recommend with any enthusiasm. If I wanted to buy a sickle and could not find a congenial tool at a yard sale or auction and did not know a smith who could pound out the shape I like, I would choose as an alternative the light-weight Japanese sickle-kama sold by Smith and Hawken. The kama also comes in heavy and medium-weight models. The light one does the same work as the sickle, and though it weighs only 8 ounces, the additional leverage supplied by the long handle (18 inches) compensates for the lack of weight. The long handle lets you reach in under overhanging shrubs, and you can do some cutting chores without having either to kneel or bend way over, as you must with a regular sickle. The kama's one drawback is the smooth, slim handle, which I found constantly slithering out of my hand. Perhaps a handle wrapping would take care of that problem.

The medium and heavy-weight kamas are, I feel, too much tool for trimming light grass and weeds, and far too little for any serious mucking out. "Serious" is both quantitative and qualitative. It suggests any area large enough to keep you nibbling away interminably with a sickle or any adversary tough enough to stop a sickle dead in its tracks. For such jobs a scythe is the only sensible tool, and by far the best one around is the Austrian-style scythe originally promoted and sold in this country by David Tresemer at Green River Tools (now out of business). The snath, or scythe handle, is light; its design lets you stand comfortably as you work; and the weight of the tool is forward in the blade, where it belongs. Equipped with what Tresemer called the "grass-and-grain" blade (28 inches long), this scythe is the ideal tool for dealing with those edges and transitional areas on a country place or even a large house lot where you don't want to tend a lawn but do want to keep the weeds and grass down: the roadside, the borders of a long driveway, that patch out behind the garage and the clothesline.

If I see anything tougher than heavy weeds coming, I exchange the grass-and-grain blade for a 22-inch bush blade. Leverage can work against you as well as for you, and whipping the relatively long grass-and-grain blade into a dense raspberry patch puts undue strain both on the snath and on its user. The bush blade is easier to maneuver in thick growth, and its shorter cutting edge means that you can slice through heavier stuff with the same application of power. A bush blade will handle that raspberry patch easily, and it will even let you slash through hardhack.

Just how heavy a sapling a bush blade will handle is a moot point. It will zip through an isolated softwood stem (pine, alder) about half an inch thick, but an oak sapling of the same diameter may bring it to a jarring halt. If you find yourself unable to nip off a sapling by setting the base of the blade near the snath against it and giving one firm, easy pull, then it is best to put the scythe aside and reach for a billhook.

With this tool, you grasp the sapling in one hand, bend it toward you, set the hook against the bent stem as close to the ground as possible, then pull back with a smooth, slicing motion. To work properly, the hook must indeed be a *bill*hook shaped like a hawk's bill. If the hook is too open, it slides off, rather than slicing through, the stem. The "Woodsman's Pal," available from Survival Equipment Company of Oley, Pennsylvania, is a sturdy tool with a proper billhook on one side of the blade and a cutting edge that can be used like a hatchet on the other. I much prefer the model that has a wooden handle to the one with the leather grip and handguard.

Because brush cutting requires a greater output of energy than grass trimming, the option of a machine driven by a gasoline engine may be even more appealing here. However, you do not have to be a brute to wield a brush scythe effectively. I stand 5 feet 8 inches and weigh 145 pounds and I suspect there are many

Swiss and Austrian farmers two-thirds my size who can mow me into the ground. Unless you are facing acre upon acre to clear, I see no reason for any healthy, reasonably vigorous individual to invest in a power brush cutter.

All these hand tools, of course, are only as good as their edges are sharp. The scythe stone you use to touch up your scythe will also do nicely for the sickle, but if your hand slips when sharpening a sickle, the tight curve of the blade will make a nasty cut almost inevitable. Use extreme caution, and a pair of heavy leather gloves. The blade can be kept steady by driving the tip into a log or fence post. The danger of cutting yourself while using a scythe or sickle is slight. The direction of the cut with the sickle is across the body, not toward it; and the length of the snath keeps the scythe blade away from your ankles. These tools are a much greater hazard if you leave them lying in the grass, forget them, then walk into them. Worse yet is a scythe hung over a tree branch at about eye or throat level.

Well sharpened, this repertoire of tools will handle all the clearing jobs most gardeners are ever likely to face. But if you find you've run through your entire arsenal and your adversary will not yield even to a billhook, then perhaps you have slid from large-scale brush into small-scale trees, and it may be time to move up to a saw, an axe, and a big blue ox.

Scythe Sources

Along with the Austrian-style snath, Green River Tools used to offer four different scythe blades imported from Austria, a peening hammer, a portable anvil, whetstones, and David Tresemer's very readable treatise on the history and use of the scythe, *The Scythe Book*.

Now, you have to go to Smith and Hawken, 25 Corte Madera, Mill Valley, California 94941. They carry the same Vermont-made ash snath and all the other accessories, including Tresemer's book. However, Smith and Hawken offer only one blade, a 29½-inch grass blade also made in Austria and, I am told, of a quality comparable with the Sensen-Union blades formerly sold by Green River.

On my rather jungly Maine farm a bush blade is an absolute necessity, and I'm happy to say that they are still available in this country through the Green Earth Tool Company, 22 Douglass Street, Keene, New Hampshire 03431. Green Earth still carries two Sensen-Union blades—the 28-inch grass-and-grain blade and the 22-inch bush blade.

A. M. Leonard, Inc., Piqua, Ohio 45356, has a straight Austrian-style snath and a 30-inch Austrian Swan brand blade, neither of which I have had a chance to use.

The Yard Hydrant

For many winters I watered my small flock of sheep the hard way. The hard way is to fill two buckets with water in the kitchen, then go staggering out the door at 6 A.M., slip on the ice, drop both buckets, soak your pantlegs, go back inside, refill the buckets, go back out the door, carefully circumvent the ice patch, wallow through knee-deep snow the fifty yards to the sheep shed, stumble in a hip-deep drift halfway there and lose one bucket, continue on with the other, leave it with the sheep, pick up the two buckets you left for them last night, head back to the house, snaring the spilled bucket out of the snow drift on the way, put last night's two ice-caked buckets near the stove to thaw, fill your one remaining bucket, take it back down to the sheep shed, come back to the house, and change your wet clothes. Repeat this routine at least morning, noon, and night each day, more often on bitter cold days when the buckets ice over quickly.

There had to be a better way, and I found it. The idea is to have a pipe carry the water instead of carrying it by hand yourself. Fine, but once you've dug your ditch, laid your black plastic pipe below the frost line, and tapped into your household water supply, how do you run the water up into an unheated barn or shed or to an outdoor watering trough without the exposed pipe and faucet freezing in the winter? The answer is a simple device known as a yard hydrant.

The main body of the yard hydrant is a length of 1-inch galvanized pipe with a shut-off valve at one end and a faucet operated by a lever handle at the other. When you lift the handle, a brass rod that runs down inside the galvanized pipe raises the plunger in the shut-off valve buried below frost level, letting water run up through the pipe and out the faucet. Conversely, when you lower the handle, the rod drops the plunger back down onto the valve seat and shuts the flow of water off underground. Also, once the plunger is reseated, it leaves a bleeder hole in the side of the valve body open so that the water in the standpipe can drain out into the ground. The pipe and faucet never contain any standing water that can freeze.

Because the yard hydrant is not a pump, it can be used only on water lines that are themselves under pressure from a pump or a gravity-feed system. It is also crucial that the hydrant be installed with the valve end below the frost line. Yard hydrants come in different lengths that let you bury the valve anywhere from 1 to 8 feet below ground level while leaving twenty-six inches of standpipe above ground.

In areas where frost depth reaches several feet, use a small backhoe to dig a narrow trench for the water pipe to the nearest source of pressurized water. If that source happens to be in your cellar, drill a hole through the foundation wall. This work may cost several hundred dollars, depending on depth, type of soil, length of pipe, and local labor prices.

It's best to err on the conservative side and bury your line and valve a little too deep rather than a little too shallow. In my part of Maine, water lines are usually installed 5 feet underground. One hydrant maker, the Simmons Manufacturing Company of McDonough, Georgia, recommends you dig down 6 feet if you're on a latitude with St. Paul, Minnesota; 5 feet, with Chicago; and 4 feet, with St. Louis. Latitude alone is not a reliable guide, however, because local temperatures and snow cover can vary greatly from year to year. So install your water line and hydrant valve deep enough to survive the maximum frost depth of a double-whammy winter, that is, one with no snow cover at all and the lowest possible temperatures for your area. (Snow acts as a blanket, insulating the soil against sub-zero temperatures.) The best bet is to check with your local water department or well drillers.

It's important, too, that the valve be able to drain freely. If it is just buried in the dirt, the bleeder hole may become clogged. To insure proper drainage, install the lower end of the hydrant in what amounts to a small dry well. The hole in which you set the hydrant should be about two feet in diameter, and you should fill the bottom of it two feet deep with crushed stone or coarse gravel.

The Simmons hydrant is available in two models, the 4800 and 800. The only difference between them is that the 800 series has a hand wheel on it that lets you set the flow of water at whatever rate you want from a mere trickle to full blast. The 4800 locks only in the on or off position. The hand wheel adds only a few dollars to the price. A 4800 hydrant with a bury depth of 6 feet lists for $84.34. The list price for the same size in the 800 model with the locking wheel is $88.82.

The pistol-grip handle on either model can be padlocked to the hydrant head. This feature does more, I am told, than prevent tampering by human hands. A horse owner reports that one of his animals not only learned to operate the lever but also learned to pull out a stick the man had put through the locking holes. This horseman now has a padlock on his hydrant and is keeping the key to it carefully hidden from his horses.

The yard hydrant is not limited to keeping livestock supplied with water year round. It can also be of great help to a gardener. A faucet adapter (list price $4.50) accepts any standard garden hose coupling, and if you locate a yard hydrant near your garden, you are not only spared wrestling with miles of hose every time you want to water the garden, but you also get a heavier flow closer to where you want it. And when winter comes, there are no surface pipes or faucets you have to remember to drain.

Yard hydrants are available nationwide from hardware stores and from plumbing and pump-and-well suppliers. They are also sold under the Harvard brand name and are available from Sears and W. W. Granger. You can expect to pay well below list prices. Sears Farm and Ranch catalogue, for example, has an 800 model with a bury depth of three feet for $42.47 and one with a bury depth of five feet for $46.45. A local dealer in my area offered prices about 20 percent below list.

Knowing Your Ropes

When I was a child, my mother's response to just about any preposterous or outrageous tale I would tell her was "Go smoke a rope," an expression akin to "Go jump in the lake" or "Go soak your head." I had always assumed that smoking a rope would be a pretty unpleasant business, but now that I know a little bit more about rope, I'm not so sure. Hemp is derived from the stalks of *Cannabis sativa,* better known to you and me as marijuana; and for many centuries, perhaps even for milennia, hemp was the world's primary rope material. Ships in the Mediterranean were rigged with hemp rope as early as 200 B.C., and Chinese tradition has it that the emperor Shen Nung was promoting the cultivation of hemp back in the 28th century B.C. Whether Shen Nung was interested in rope or in dope is not entirely clear, and I also wonder now if my mother was really suggesting I smoke a rope or take a toke.

If your primary interest in rope is smoking it, you're out of luck these days. Hemp rope lost a large share of the world market as early as the 1830s when American ropemakers turned to the much harder abaca fiber, grown in the Philippines. Manila rope made from that fiber would remain the world standard until it was dethroned by nylon in the 1950s. Manila still has its virtues. It is very abrasion resistant, and it neither loses strength nor swells when wet. But when the fibers dry out, which they do relatively quickly on extended exposure to the weather, the rope loses its strength.

Also, even when new, manila is no match for nylon. A ½-inch three-strand nylon rope, weighing only 6½ pounds per 100 feet, has a breaking strength of 5,750 pounds. Three-strand manila has to be 13/16-inch, weighing 19½ pounds per 100 feet, to reach a comparable breaking strength (5,850 pounds). The reductions in weight and bulk that nylon allows are obvious, not to mention the greater durability and greater resistance to most chemicals. You'll still find natural-fiber cordage, like small manila and sisal ropes and jute twine, in your local hardware store, and cotton continues to be used in some clotheslines and sash cord, but in ropes for marine use, tree work, utility work, and general hauling and hoisting, the synthetics now dominate the market.

Nylon was the first artificial fiber to be widely utilized in rope, and it remains the standard against which the properties of other synthetics are measured. Its major characteristics are high strength per unit weight, minimal loss of strength on exposure to sunlight, and excellent resistance to rot, mildew, and abrasion. Along with high strength, nylon's most important working property is its elasticity. Depending on the construction methods used in them, nylon ropes will stretch roughly 10 percent at normal working loads and up to about 40 percent at 75 percent of the breaking load. This quality makes nylon the fiber of choice for "dynamic ropes" used in mountain climbing because it absorbs the energy of a fall and so reduces the impact on the human body.

Polyester (DuPont's trade name is Dacron) shares most of nylon's virtues but differs from it in having low elasticity. Because it does not stretch as much, it is often a component in the mountaineer's "static ropes," used for rappelling or in rescue work where energy absorption is not important and elongation under load is a disadvantage. Polyester ropes generally have a slightly lower breaking or tensile strength than nylon.

The third synthetic fiber and the most popular one today, primarily because of its low cost, is polypropylene. If you compare a manila and a polypro rope of the same size, the polypro is half again as strong, one-third lighter, and far more durable. With a specific gravity of .91, it floats and is therefore handy for many boating, beach, and swimming pool uses. But polypro rope is only about two-thirds as strong as nylon or polyester. It is also very prone to ultraviolet degradation and can lose 50 percent of its strength at a temperature as low as 150° F. Because of its lower initial strength and its susceptibility to degradation, polypropylene should not be used where life, limb, or valuable property will depend on it. But for noncritical uses, such as lashing down tarps, boat covers, and so forth, it is an appropriate and economical choice. The monofilament polypropylene found in most stores is stiff, wiry, kinky stuff that does not handle or knot well and that splinters with use, making it hard on the hands. Multifilament polypropylene (known in the industry as MFP) uses much finer fibers than the monofilament to produce a softer, more flexible rope that is still low in price.

If cost were never an object and I didn't have a special need for a floating rope, I would choose nylon or polyester for any use, critical or not, making my choice between the two dependent on whether elasticity or relatively low elasticity was desirable for the application I had in mind. Both these ropes have a good hand, which they do not lose with use; they knot easily; and they are long-lived if properly cared for. If you foresee use that requires a lot of handling, tying, and untying, nylon and polyester may well be worth the significantly higher price you'll pay for them. And the price can run close to two or three times higher. In my local Agway, a 50-foot roll of three-strand, 3/8-inch polypro costs $5.99, or 12 cents a foot; smaller nylon (5/16-inch) is 20 cents a foot. Or to compare another way, the suggested retail prices for 600 feet of New England Ropes' three-strand, 1/2-inch rope in nylon, filament Dacron, and polypropylene are $288, $360, and $126 respectively.

Given those price differences, it's easy to see why polypro remains popular for noncritical applications and why manila and sisal, which are modestly priced, too, are still on the shelves. But if your life is quite literally on the line, as it is for an arborist or mountain climber, or if you have to lower a harpsicord from a fourth-floor window, the prices of nylon and polyester don't look so high after all.

In addition to these commonly used fibers, some super-fibers have also found their way into rope, particularly in marine applications. Ropes made with DuPont's Kevlar and Allied Corporation's Spectra, an olefin fiber, are seven and ten times stronger than steel for their respective weights. Their great strength and near zero stretch make these ropes ideal for sailboat stays or if you want to give someone enough rope to hang himself. The prices of these ropes are, however, every bit as amazing as their qualities, quarter-inch lines going at about a dollar per foot.

Three-strand rope is what most people will probably think of when they hear the word "rope." It is the cheapest manufacturing process and produces a rope with good bulk and a knobby texture that allows a firm grip on it. In this construction, long fibers are typically twisted together clockwise into yarns, counterclockwise into thicker strands, and finally clockwise again into rope. The opposing twists and the friction between the fibers resist stretching and unraveling. However, under enough strain a three-strand rope does tend to unwind. The more expensive 12-strand braid produces a rope that cannot unwind or kink. Double braided ropes combine a braided core with a braided cover, allowing various fibers and types of braiding to be combined to produce certain desired qualities. Like twelve-strand, they will not unwind either. Given the same material and same rope size, three-strand rope will stretch the most; twelve-strand braid, less; and double braid, least. The core-and-cover principle permits other variations, too. A common one used often in clothesline and other ropes as well is a core made of straight fibers with a cover braided over it.

The first step in using ropes safely is to select the right rope for the job it will do. Strength is the major consideration but not the only one. Reels and packages of rope are usually marked either with the average tensile (breaking) strength or with the working load of the rope. The two are *not* the same. The Cordage Institute defines the working load as the *minimum* breaking strength divided by a figure the Institute calls the "safety factor." The safety factor differs for different rope diameters and materials. Some typical working loads will run about 10 to 20 percent of the tensile strength. For instance, a 3/8-inch polyester rope with a tensile strength of 3,340 pounds and a safety factor of 10 will have a working load of 340 pounds. That working load applies only for new rope under static load, not dynamic loads (such as the shock load a falling mountaineer puts on a rope) or sustained loads (keeping the rope under working load for a long time). Load should always be put on a rope slowly and smoothly to avoid shock loading that could exceed the rope's tensile strength. Ropes that have been subject to shock or sustained elongation will be weakened and should be either discarded or downrated.

Other factors that weaken synthetic ropes are extended exposure to sunlight and heat (polypropylene being the most sensitive to both), so rope should always be stored in a clean, dry, well-ventilated place away from direct sunlight and extreme heat. Heat generated from friction can be just as damaging. Unlike natural fibers, the synthetics are rot- and mildew-proof and resistant to most chemicals, but they still should not be stored wet or together with acids or alkalies. Check with the manufacturer about chemical sensitivies. Abrasion from dirt, concrete floors, sharp edges, or rusted winches will also weaken ropes. Examine your ropes often for frayed external fibers; separate the strands and look for powdery internal fibers. If you have any doubts about a rope, downgrade it, discard it, or, if you can't stand to see it go to waste, put it in your pipe and smoke it.

Information about Rope

Most hardware and farm-supply retailers carry limited selections of rope. You may have better luck at a marina, but even there you may find only a few specialized marine ropes. The Cordage Institute, 42 North Street, Hingham, Massachusetts 02043, 617-749-1016, is the national association of the rope industry and a good place to ask any and all questions you may have about rope. Manufacturers' catalogs will give you concise overviews of rope characteristics and strengths, and you can inquire directly of their customer service divisions for help in choosing the specific rope you may need and in locating a distributor near you who carries it. A few addresses are:

Lambeth Corporation, P.O. Box G-825, New Bedford, Massachusetts 02742, 617-995-2626.

New England Ropes, Pope's Island, New Bedford, Massachusetts 02740, 617-999-2351.

Samson Ocean Systems, Inc., P.O. Box 638, Shirley, Massachusetts 01464, 800-227-7673.

The *Samson Rope Manual* (available from Samson for $10) contains general information on rope characteristics and uses and is also recognized throughout the industry as the bible of detailed, technical information on rope.

A book that will both introduce you to ropes and show you how to work with them is Barbara Merry, *Splicing Handbook: Techniques for Modern and Traditional Ropes*, $11.95 postpaid from the International Marine Publishing Company, 21 Elm Street, Camden, Maine 04843.

A Handle on Rakes

Raking up around the yard is a chore I regard as a kind of outdoor housework. The process is repetitive and not particularly edifying, but the results amply reward the effort. The carpet of maple leaves in October, attractive enough when it first falls, will turn into a sodden, grass-smothering mat if left to itself. And in the spring, a brisk once-over with the lawn rake picks the dead thatch out of the lawn, aerates it, gets rid of the gravel tossed up by the snowplow, and peels up those sodden leaves you missed last fall.

Not only does raking yield the benefits of beauty and order, it also yields good stuff for the compost heap: leaves, dead grass, sawdust, rotting twigs and bark. And it is outdoor activity at two of the year's sweetest times: the last warm days before snow comes and that first powerful surge of spring when the snow has been gone for only a few days, and the earth starts to rise like bread in the heat of the sun.

Now that I start thinking about it, of course, raking begins to look like a lot more fun than housework, how much more depending in part on the weather you choose to do it in and on the tool you choose to do it with. A lawn rake would appear to be a simple enough device, but the many designs and sizes of rakes available suggest that the truly perfect lawn rake has yet to be invented.

The furthest ones from perfection, in my experience, are the steel-tine rakes, whether the tines are made from flat spring steel or round wire. I've seen the wire-tined variety described as "leaf rakes" as opposed to "lawn rakes" because the wire tines tear the grass and hang up in it. But a leaf rake that cannot rake up leaves on a lawn strikes me as a severely limited tool, particularly when there are other rakes that pick up leaves better on any terrain. So strike the wire-tined rakes.

A great deal of ingenuity has gone into designs for the flat-tined rakes. They come in fan shapes and with straight edges. They come large and they come small. They come with shorter tines and longer tines. They come with and without reinforcing springs to increase tension on the tines. All for nought. Even when made of high-quality spring steel, as the better models are, steel-tine rakes are still quite lifeless. They lack bounce and quick rebound. They feel heavy and unresponsive in the hand. And though they do not tangle in the grass as badly as wire rakes, they still tend to hang up more than is desirable. So strike the flat-tined steel rakes, too.

The reason why steel makes such a poor lawn rake is, I suspect, because a lawn rake is not really a rake at all but rather a cross between a rake and a broom. When you rake leaves or grass clippings, you hold the lawn rake like a broom and use it like a broom, sweeping rather than raking. You may occasionally turn both hands downward to claw at a stubborn patch of wet leaves, but most of the time you hold the rake upright, palms facing each other, and sweep. And the action you want from the tool is part grabbing, part whisking.

The traditional material that has done that job best is bamboo, and bamboo lawn rakes are still a staple item in hardware and lawn-and-garden stores. I hope they always will be, because a bamboo rake has many virtues. It manages to reach down into the grass to pick up leaves and debris, yet it does not snag. It flexes readily, following the contours of rough, lumpy lawns like mine. Its springy action lets you half push, half fling great heaps of leaves ahead of you. If you give it reasonable care and use it only for what it is meant to do—that is, rake the lawn—it will last longer than its fragile appearance would suggest. If you don't run your car over your rake, use it for a snow shovel, or pull its teeth out on a chain-link fence, it may well be with you for five years or more. I know of one bamboo rake still alive after twelve years. And even if you do ruin your rake, it's no tragedy. Bamboo is a renewable resource, and rake-making keeps people gainfully employed in a nonpolluting industry. Also, bamboo rakes are so modestly priced that no one will go broke replacing one occasionally.

The George W. McGuire Company of Whitestone, New York, has been making fine bamboo rakes since 1919. McGuire rakes, unlike the imports from Taiwan, are assembled in this country. The bamboo is carefully sorted, and poor quality tines are discarded. The clamps are heavy duty, the handles, thicker and sturdier than on the discount-store competition. The McGuire label rakes come in three sizes, 18-, 24-, and 30-inch, and retail at about $6, $8, and $10 respectively. The 30-inch rake covers the most ground in the least time and is the only lawn rake I feel I need. If you want to do a more thorough job of thatching your lawn in the spring, you might find the 18-inch rake with its finer teeth (31 in the rake's 18-inch span) a handy supplementary tool.

I have a strong prejudice for natural materials over synthetic ones, for the product made from renewable resources over one made from nonrenewable resources; but when it comes to lawn rakes, I have to concede that polypropylene makes a very good rake indeed.

Ames' polypropylene rakes, called Greensweepers, come in the same sizes as bamboo rakes. Suggested retail prices on the 24- and 30-inch sizes are $9.90 and $9.80, on the 18-inch one, $8.10. The design of the Greensweeper lends both firmness and flex to the material, and while the resulting action may not exceed that of bamboo, it certainly comes very close to it. The somewhat livelier and more independent action of the tines in a bamboo rake may make it better for thatching, but the Greensweeper is every bit as good as a leaf rake. If it becomes clogged with leaves, the slippery plastic tines can easily be cleaned by just turning the rake over and swiping its back across the grass. Then, too, the Greensweeper is lighter, hence less tiring to use.

A large lawn rake is fine for sweeping the lawn, but what do you use to claw leaves out from under and between your azaleas, rhododendrons, lilacs, or what-have-you? A wide lawn rake won't fit between the stems of shrubs growing close together, and if you try to force the issue, you'll get hung up, break tines, and go quietly crazy at the same time. Metal-tined rakes fare no better than bamboo or polypro. Their tines just bend before they break, and the frustration quotient is just as large.

Rake-makers offer what they call "shrub rakes" to fill the gap. Available in steel (Union Fork and Hoe), polypropylene (Ames, True Temper), and bamboo (McGuire), shrub rakes range from 6 to 11 inches wide and have 7 to 15 tines. Narrower of head and shorter of tine as they are, these rakes can wiggle into tight places more easily than their larger cousins and therefore represent something of an improvement. If the quarters you're working in are not too tight, you won't get hung up; but if you're trying to dig leaves from between tightly arrayed woody stems, you're bound to get snagged and will soon have bent and broken tines. Alternatives to flexible-tined rakes are 3- or 4-pronged cultivators or the small 6- or 7-tined garden rakes the manufacturers call "floral rakes." These, too, will hang up in the thickets, but at least you can yank on them and put some pressure on them without bending them all out of shape. The truth of the matter is that I have yet to find the tool that will accomplish this particular task with ease and grace.

Adjustable broom rakes try to be all things to all users. They have a sliding collar on the handle that lets you retract the tines through a fixed cross piece, thus narrowing the rake to shrub rake width. When you push the collar down the handle, the rake fans out to small lawn-rake size. The wire-tined model I tested (brand name: A-Just-O-Rake) had much too short a handle and was so flimsy it started bending after ten minutes of use. Other makes may be sturdier, but I still feel you'll be much better served by two separate tools.

Finally, no discussion of lawn rakes can properly end without mention of the Rugg Model 39 Lawn Rake, which retails for $14.29 at my local farmers' union. This is not in fact a lawn rake if by that you mean a flexible-tined, broom-style rake like all those mentioned above. The Model 39 looks rather like an oversized wooden garden rake. The head consists of a 28-inch wide crossbar in which twenty-eight 3¾-inch wooden teeth are embedded. Wire hoops and a metal ferrule link the cross bar to the handle, providing strength and stability. The Model 39 is in fact a descendant of the old longer-toothed wooden hay rakes that were used in the days before horse- or tractor-drawn hay rakes. I use this rake not for raking leaves or grass clippings but for the many mini-haying jobs I have around my place: small areas that won't admit mechanized haying equipment and that I mow once or twice a season with a scythe and rake with the Model 39. The tool is light, the teeth are angled for easy raking, and the reinforcing hoops aid in rolling the grass into windrows that you can then pick up with a pitchfork and cart and use for mulching the garden or for composting.

Long, Thin Buckets

Times were when "garden hose" meant a black, rubber hose, and that was that. Now, in the age of plastics and synthetic fibers, there is a much wider range of hoses designed for home, farm, and garden use, many of them in spiffy colors an interior decorator might drool over. There are hoses that wear wide nylon mesh pretty enough for a pair of stockings. There are yellow-striped hoses that look like 50-foot garter snakes. There are emerald-green jobs that could double as dragon skin.

Gardening writer Jim Crockett cites a snippet of country wisdom that says a hose is nothing but a long, thin bucket; and just as a big bucket will move more water faster than a small one, so it is with hoses. The most common inside diameters of garden hoses are ½- and ⅝-inch. That ⅛-inch difference may not sound or look like much, but where 100 feet of ½-inch hose at the usual household water pressure of 40 pounds per square inch (psi) will deliver six gallons in one minute, a ⅝-inch hose will deliver eleven gallons and a ¾-inch hose, eighteen gallons. There is no point in buying ½-inch hose unless you have some specific reason for wanting to deliver water at a slower rate. "Garden hose" typically means ⅝-inch, and that diameter combines relative ease in handling with delivery of a large enough volume of water for most household and garden needs. However, to keep water volume up at distances of 100 feet or more from faucet to delivery point, you may want to use ¾-inch either for the whole run or in your first length of hose from the faucet.

Hose is ordinarily sold in lengths of 25, 50, 75, and 100 feet, though you will find some hoses in 30-foot increments, "80-foot specials," and so on. Fifty-footers are the longest snakes I care to wrestle with, and 25-footers are twice as easy to handle and drain. If, for example, the longest run you would ever need is 100 feet, you're better off with four 25-foot lengths (or one 50 and two 25's) than with a 100 or two 50's. Along with greater convenience, the shorter lengths give you greater efficiency, too. Because volume delivered per minute drops as the length of the hose increases, three 25-foot lengths coupled together are more efficient for a target 75 feet from the tap than two 50-foot lengths would be. You will, however, pay somewhat more for those benefits. The shorter the length of any hose, the higher the per-foot price is.

The ideal hose material should be durable and resistant to abrasion and cuts. It should be able to withstand sub-zero temperatures and scorching heat. It should be soft enough to flex well, yet it should be stiff enough not to kink. It should have high burst resistance, so that when you shut the nozzle off and leave the hose cooking in the hot sun, it won't blow out on you. It should be light enough for a child to handle easily. And, of course, it should be moderately priced.

That adds up to a tall order, but many hose materials (usually combinations of materials) come close to filling it, some being stronger in one respect, some in another. Nonreinforced vinyl, usually labeled "100% vinyl, 2-ply garden hose," is cheap (about $4 for 50 feet of ½-inch) and lightweight, but it is otherwise an embarrassment even to the folks who make it. Don't buy it, but don't be scared off by "vinyl" either, because there are many respectable vinyl hoses on the market.

These reinforced vinyl hoses all use the same basic three-part construction method: (1) an inside tube that carries the water, (2) nylon or polyester reinforcing mesh, (3) an outer "skin" to protect the reinforcement. The strength, durability, flexibility, and resistance to kinking are determined in part by the quality of the plastics used in each hose and by the type of reinforcement. Spiral reinforcement is a synthetic thread wound one way around the core tube. Dual spiral adds another thread wound on in the opposite direction. (This is the "belted radial" pattern also used in tires.) Braided reinforcement looks like spiral, but the threads are interwoven rather than simply wound one on top of the other. Knit reinforcement looks like a more or less wide-mesh knitted fabric. The strength of the reinforcement depends more on the concentration of it and on the thickness of the threads than on the type. A tight knit of heavy thread, for example, will be stronger than a loose knit of light thread. For even greater strength, better quality hoses use dual reinforcement, often combining knit and spiral. Because many vinyl hoses have transparent outer covers, you can see the reinforcement; and even with opaque covers, the reinforcement pattern is often visible through the skin. Then, too, the manufacturer's label or catalog will usually tell you what kind of reinforcing is used in a particular hose.

Apart from reinforcement, the consumer's other clues to quality are the couplings, the price, and the manufacturer's own ratings. Any of Swan's garden hoses, for example, will be rated good, better, or best with two, three, or five stars on the label (Reinforced Quality, All-Weather Quality, and Premium Quality). Colorite is currently using a rebate tag that identifies good, better, and best by style number. Top-line hoses will have machined brass couplings, which you can recognize by the octagonal shape. Some (Colorite, Gates) also add a protective collar to help prevent kinking at the coupling. "Better" hoses often have a rubber or plastic easy-grip device molded to a lighter brass fitting. And the "good" hose will have just the light, spun-brass couplings. Typical prices for a 50-foot, ⅝-inch reinforced vinyl hose in the three grades will run about $14, $11, and $8 respectively.

I have used a medium-grade knit-reinforced hose (Teknor

Apex's "SuperFlex") for several years now, and at the price it is hard to beat. It's light, easy to handle, and has stood up well to frequent though not hard use. I should add, however, that my water pressure is quite low. If you're on a municipal water system that may deliver pressures up to 100 psi, you'll want a better grade hose with high burst resistance.

What are reinforced vinyl's limits and disadvantages? Under normal use and pressures, practically none. However, it will suffer from extremes of temperatures. Exposed to −20° F or lower, it will crack if flexed (it can be stored safely at those temperatures). And at temperatures of 120° F or above, the plasticizers in even better-grade vinyls will leach out, and the hose will deteriorate. In other words, don't give your vinyl hose a sun bath in Death Valley. And if you like to flood skating rinks in Maine winters (as I sometimes do), then you might want to look for a different hose material.

For ability to withstand extreme temperatures (from about −40° F to 160° or 180°), for greatest cut and abrasion resistance, and for overall long life, 100 percent rubber hose is the choice. Rubber hose, too, uses the three-layer construction, but here the inside tube and the skin are both pure rubber. The disadvantages of all rubber are weight and higher price. Fifty feet of ⅝-inch will weigh about nine pounds as opposed to seven for the best reinforced vinyl and five for better grade. And the price is around $25. For the gardener who will give a hose moderate use in moderate temperatures, 100 percent rubber is probably overkill.

A construction that tries to combine rubber's ruggedness and durability with vinyl's ease of handling is—as you might expect—the rubber/vinyl hose. Prices I've seen for 50 feet of top-quality ⅝-inch go from about $16 for Swan's "Soft and Supple" or Colorite's "Rubber + Vinyl" to about $25 for Gates' "Flexogen." Skeptics claim the durability is not as good as with 100 percent rubber, but given the price, the sweet handling, and the lifetime guarantees that go with these premium hoses, I think I'd be willing to take a chance.

What Do Hoses Really Cost?

The prices I've been quoting here are what are usually listed on tags as "regular" or "suggested" prices, but what you will actually have to pay may be quite different. You may well find the same quality hose going for several dollars less in a high-volume, low-overhead store than it does in your corner hardware store.

Also, many hose manufacturers offer rebates that apply regardless of the retailer's asking price. Rebates range from $3 on top-line hoses down to $1 on "good" grades. However, those guidelines are not ironclad, and you may find higher rebates.

As an example of the kind of savings you may find, particularly on promotional lengths of hose, I came across 80 feet of ⅝-inch Teknor Apex Hi-Flex, a knit-reinforced vinyl hose, with a "regular" price of $17.99. The sale price, however, was $11.97, and if you cared to take advantage of the $3 rebate, the hose was yours for $8.97.

In short, the prices on even the best hoses are modest; and if you shop carefully, you can make them more modest still.

Some Major Manufacturers of Garden Hose

ANCHOR SWAN
P.O. Box 609
Worthington, Ohio 43085

COLORITE PLASTICS COMPANY
Ridgefield, New Jersey 07657

GATES RUBBER COMPANY
Box 5887
Denver, Colorado 80217

MOORE MANUFACTURING, INC.
San Francisco, California 94134

TEKNOR APEX COMPANY
Pawtucket, Rhode Island 02862

Making Your Own Cider

Cider-making is a rural chore so close to pure pleasure that to call it "work" seems almost blasphemous. The first step—going out to gather apples—is hardly an onerous task. It's a privilege just to be outdoors on a sunny, fall afternoon when the hills are ablaze with color and the air as crisp and tangy as a first bite into a Northern Spy. Add to that the pleasure of exploring old orchards, finding some apple varieties you know and some you don't, and coming home with a few grain sacks stuffed with apples and redolent with their perfume.

Then the actual pressing of the cider, whether you do it as a family or join forces with several neighbors, always has the quality of a festival. Kids, dogs, adults—everybody can get into the act. It's fun to blast the apples with a hose, roll them into the hopper, and grind them to pomace for that first pressing. And when you wind the screw of the press down, the whole crew drops whatever they may be doing and gathers, cups in hand, to catch and sample the rush of amber nectar. If ever there was a distillate of the sweetness and zest of October, it is surely to be found in that first taste of cider; and the mood that comes over the drinkers is at once one of gaiety and near-religious celebration.

The basic tools of cidering are a press and a grinder. Perhaps the presses most appropriate for a home operation are the single-tub, screw presses like the Jaffrey Cider and Wine Press and the Happy Valley Ranch "Homesteader." They cost $335 and $339 respectively, plus shipping, and may also be purchased as ready-to-assemble kits ($315 and $319) or as hardware-only kits ($169 and $229).

Both the Happy Valley Ranch and the Jaffrey presses have tubs large enough to process about a bushel of apples at each pressing and, depending on the juice content of the apples, to yield about 2 to 2½ gallons of cider. Small tabletop presses meant for soft fruits are not adequate for even a small cider operation. Happy Valley Ranch's double-tub "American Harvester" press ($489) lets you fill one tub with pomace while you're pressing juice from the other. In all three presses, the tubs are slotted to let the juice run out the sides; and before loading the pulp into the tubs, you line them with fine nylon-mesh pressing bags that let the juice flow through but prevent seeds, stems, and skin from making their way into the cider. All three presses also come equipped with grinders, which are mounted over the tubs and let you grind the pomace directly into the tub. Or, if you want to continue grinding while you press with the single tub presses, the grinders can be taken off and mounted separately. Improved grinders on the latest models produce a finer pomace, which in turn produces increased yields-per-pressing. Another simple device, which you can buy from Jaffrey for $18 or make yourself, is a wooden grate to place under the tub and pressing bag. Because it enables you to press the bag out almost dry rather than leaving it puddling in its own juice, it too increases the yield.

The Bess Company makes a small, home-scale version of the large rack-and-cloth presses used in commercial operations. The rack-and-cloth system plus the hydraulic cylinders used in these presses increase the yield from a given amount of apples; however, the price for Bess's smallest model (the 38) is somewhat higher ($418 for press and grinder), and operation is slower.

In addition to your press and grinder, you'll need a container to catch the cider as it drains from the press. Glass or an odorless plastic are good materials, and you can also use stainless steel or unchipped enamelware. Do not use any containers made of galvanized metal, aluminum, copper, other metals, or chipped enamelware. The acid in apple juice eats into these metals, and your cider will quickly take on a metallic taste. The same rule applies to any other utensils you may need. Use plastic scoops, funnels, etc.

You can store sweet cider by freezing it in plastic jugs or waxed cardboard containers, but leave some air space for expansion during freezing if you do. A method more saving of freezer space is to pasteurize the cider and keep it in your root cellar or pantry. Pasteurization takes some of the tangy edge off freshly pressed cider; but if the cider has been made from a lively blend of apples, your homemade pasteurized cider will still be a far tastier beverage than commercial apple juice. To pasteurize cider, heat it in a stainless steel or unchipped enamel pot to 190° F and keep it at that temperature for two to three minutes. Then, pour the slightly cooled cider into canning jars or self-sealing glass jugs that have been sterilized in boiling water.

Making sweet cider is a pretty straightforward business, but once you decide to let some of your cider go down that long, fizzy, fermenting road to becoming hard cider, a number of new variables enter the picture. That isn't to say that you have to be a professional chemist to make a decent barrel of Old Yankee Farmer's hard cider. Old Yankee Farmers have been doing it for generations. But if you want to be able to duplicate brilliant successes and not repeat total disasters, you may well find a hydrometer handy (to measure sugar and alcohol content); and you'll want to keep records of the blends of apple varieties you have used; of the sugar content of the must; of the amount of sugar, if any, that you add; and of details and dates in your processing. Making hard cider is too noble an art to attempt to describe in a few words here; and if you're interested in trying it, by all means apprentice yourself to an old hand or consult some of the excellent literature available on it.

For any cider, of course, sweet or hard, the apples you select to put into it will determine whether the final product is dull or delightful, zingy or insipid. Most cider makers will probably agree that there are not many single-variety cider apples readily available today, that is, apples that have such a perfect balance of acid, sugar, tannin, and aromatic oils that you can press just that one variety and produce a first-rate cider. The Golden Russet is one of those apples, and I was lucky enough to find a couple of trees left on an abandoned farm back in the hills near my place. But today, most good ciders are blended from apples with different levels of acid (high, low, medium), aromatic oils, and astringency; most poor ones are made from single varieties that are plentiful on today's market but that, used alone, do not make good cider. Delicious and McIntosh, for example, produce those floods of drab cider that fill the store shelves and roadside stands in the fall. But the low-acid Delicious mixed 50/50 with nippy, high-acid Jonathans is something else again. And if you like your cider really nippy, as Jim Hixson, the president of Jaffrey Manufacturing does, then you may use Jonathans alone. If you want to be scientific about blending your cider, Annie Proulx recommends that you press your different apple varieties separately and mix the juices according to the following table, keeping records of exact proportions used:

Low Acid (*Neutral Base*)	30 to 60 percent
Tart (*Medium to High Acid*)	10 to 20 percent
Aromatic	10 to 20 percent
Astringent	5 to 20 percent

Don't be intimidated by the table. You don't *have* to have all four types; and if you're feeling less than scientific, just take a bite here and a bite there and compare. A bland apple will make a bland cider; a tart one will make tart. Together, they may make sweet music. Much of the pleasure in cider-making comes from stumbling onto the happy accident.

Keep in mind too that the quality of the apples you use is every bit as important as the varieties. As Annie Proulx wisely observes,

"Rotten apples make rotten cider." They can impart a foul or moldy taste to cider and start it on its way to vinegar before its time. Bruised and rotting apples can also develop patulin, a known carcinogen. Drops, which are a mainstay of cider making, are most likely to contain it because drops are prone to bruising and rot. However, Dr. Gil Stoewsand, Professor of Toxicology at Cornell University and the New York State Agricultural Experiment Station in Geneva, New York, stresses that while patulin is indeed a toxic substance, its existence should be no cause for panic among cider makers or for shying away from drops altogether. Simply by screening your fruit carefully, throwing out rotting apples and cutting out brown spots, the risk of patulin can be eliminated entirely.

In short, use apples that are mature, clean, and sound. Don't collect drops in cow pastures, where they can be contaminated with manure and urine, and immediately discard any that are mushy or have broken skins. Unripe apples lack the sugar of mature ones and make for poor cider, too. If you cut an apple open and find dark brown seeds, it is ripe. If the seeds are tan or whitish, it is not.

Before you grind your apples, wash them thoroughly. Jim Hixson uses a large washtub in which he has drilled half-inch holes in the bottom and sides. He puts his apples in the tub and turns the garden hose on them full blast. The holes let the dirty water and debris drain away without his having to keep emptying the tub. This is the time, too, for a last screening to get rid of any suspect fruit.

Does it all seem like a lot of work? Well, I guess it is, and no doubt you'll have to make a lot of cider before you've earned back the price of your press. But like growing a garden or raising your own beef, you don't really do it to save money or time. You do it for the sake of "economy" in the larger sense of that word; you do it for the control it gives you over your own household management and life. Because when you press your own, you can make a cider that is clean and chemical-free and that tastes just a little different and a little better each time.

Sources and Resources

Literature

Annie Proulx, *Making the Best Apple Cider,* Garden Way Publishing Bulletin A-47, 1980, available from Storey Communications, Inc., Pownal, Vermont 05261 for $1.95 plus shipping and handling. An excellent, concise introduction to cider-making that does not overwhelm the beginner with the irrelevant.

Annie Proulx and Lew Nichols, *Sweet and Hard Cider: Making It, Using It, and Enjoying It,* Garden Way Publishing (3d printing, 1988), available from Storey Communications, Inc., Pownal, Vermont 05261, for $9.95 plus shipping and handling. This is the advanced course; indispensable for anyone interested in the fine points of hard cider-making.

Presses and Supplies

BESS COMPANY
367 Pleasant Avenue
Hamburg, New York 14075
716-649-4791

In addition to the Model 38, Bess also makes a much larger hydraulically operated rack-and-cloth press with a 5-bushel capacity and yield of 17 to 20 gallons per load; price for the press alone—$1,152.

GOODNATURE PRODUCTS, INC.
P.O. Box 233
East Aurora, New York 14052
716-652-6990

Makes a large hydraulic, rack-and-cloth press, "The Roadsider," suitable for a small commercial or co-op operation. Capacity 5½ bushels; output—up to 60 gallons per hour; price for press alone—$1,550.

HAPPY VALLEY RANCH

Route 2, Box 83
Paola, Kansas 66071
913-849-3103

"Homesteader" and "American Harvester" presses and accessories.

JAFFREY MANUFACTURING COMPANY
P.O. Box 23527
Shawnee Mission, Kansas 66223
913-681-3668

Jaffrey Cider and Wine Press and accessories.

ORCHARD EQUIPMENT AND SUPPLY
Conway, Massachusetts 01341
413-369-4335

Wide range of supplies; small and large presses.

Garden Tools

When asked why he wanted to climb Mount Everest, George Leigh Mallory made his famous reply: "Because it is there." The garden tools most of us have were probably acquired on a similar principle: We went to the hardware or discount store and bought what was there. That's too bad, because the tools most stores carry are rarely of high quality. The customer buys what's on the rack, then assumes, when the tool breaks, that garden tools are like razor blades. You use them up and throw them away.

It needn't be so. You can buy high-quality garden tools, and you should. Ten or fifteen dollars more can mean the difference between a tool that will be a joy to use and will last a lifetime and one that may last only a few seasons. And very often an excellent tool will cost no more than its poor relation.

In shovels and spades, the head is attached to the handle by one of three methods. In *hollowback* shovels, a flat sheet of metal is die cut, then shaped to fit around the handle. That is the cheapest, weakest, and lightest method. For snow shovels and scoops, that is just fine. In digging tools, however, the neck is the fulcrum on which the leverage of the handle is brought to bear, and the stronger the joint is, the better. The *solid-strap* method provides the strongest joint. A single bar of metal is forged to form a head, socket, and straps that extend up the handle and are riveted in place. A very close second in strength is the *solid socket,* also called *solid shank*. Here, too, the head and socket are forged from a single bar of steel, but because the handle is simply shaped to fit the socket, tapped into place and riveted, it is much easier to replace a broken handle in a solid-socket tool. So for a combination of strength and practicality, I prefer the solid-socket design, and it is the one thing I've come to look for in any tool, be it shovel, spade, fork, rake, hoe, or hand trowel.

The long-handled, round-point shovel is not a tool I find much use for in the garden proper, but it is an indispensable digging tool around garden and yard. In their top lines, Ames, True Temper, and Union Fork and Hoe—the three major American tool manufacturers—offer good solid-socket shovels for about $35 to $40. They also carry good garden spades in the same price range, though for those quintessential horticultural tools you may want to turn to British-made tools like the Spear and Jackson line or the Bulldog spades carried by Smith and Hawken. These English tools, beautifully crafted especially for the gardener, cost no more than the American models.

If you want a solid-socket garden fork, you will have to buy a British one (Bulldog, depending on model and handle length, about $35 to $42; Spear and Jackson, about $30). Even the best American-made forks, also priced around $35, attach head to handle with the tang-and-ferrule method. A long tang on the fork head is inserted up into the handle and the handle capped with a ferrule to prevent it from splitting. An even graver flaw is that the tines on these forks are usually too weak and will bend out of shape.

When you've finished digging up your garden and are thinking about smoothing it with a rake and, later still, weeding and cultivating it, the solid-socket tool is still the route to go. My own history is full of both wobbly-headed and completely headless (or handleless) rakes. I learn slowly, but I finally do catch on. The bow rake is one of the most common designs for garden rakes, and it could not be much worse. Two curved bows come back from the head and form a double tang that is then inserted into the rake handle. The bows, which extend the head a good four to five inches beyond the end of the handle, only increase the leverage exerted on the already weak tang-and-ferrule joint. (The advertising copy may tout this as a virtue, telling you the bows add "spring" to the rake.) Before long, the head wobbles; not long after that it falls out. And it is impossible to reattach it satisfactorily.

A much better rake is the forged "level-head" rake in which the tang on the head is driven directly into the handle. Here, the quality of the metal is crucial. If it is too light or too soft, the rake will bend or break off at the tang. Fourteen- and 17-inch American-made level-head rakes of good quality cost between $20 and $25. No American manufacturer makes heavy-duty, solid-socket rakes, although they are made in Europe and can be bought from specialty garden-supply houses for between $18 and $35.

With hoes, too, a tool in which the blade, neck, and solid socket are all forged from a single bar of steel will be strongest, and American companies do offer a number of solid-socket hoes. Or the head may be mounted on the handle with a snug fitting eye, as it is in grub hoes. The variations in models of hoes are vast, and perhaps the choice of no other garden tool is so much determined by individual needs, physiques, and preferences. My own experience of hoeing is that it is divided into two functions—heavy grubbing and light weeding—for which two different types of hoes are needed and neither of which the traditional "garden hoe" serves very well. It is too light in the head for the hacking, chopping action of breaking up the soil or coping with heavy weed growth, and it is improperly angled for nipping off young weeds. For heavy weeding and cultivating, choose tools like the American Pattern Grub Hoe (about $23 from A. M. Leonard) or the similar American and Japanese hoes from Smith and Hawken ($21 to $28). These tools look like cousins to a mattock. For nipping off young weeds, there are oscillating hoes, scuffle hoes, and draw hoes.

What they all have in common is that the blade does not chop down into the ground but is pulled (or pushed, or both) just under the surface of the ground and remains level with it. One of their great virtues is that they let you work standing up straight and so spare your back the pains of hoer's hunch.

The best oscillating hoes, like the Swiss Real Stirrup Hoe, have an all-metal head and socket and cost about $18. Cheaper models, in which the oscillating head is not hinged but just wobbles around in metal brackets, sell for about $12. In draw hoes, Gardener's Supply Company (GSC) has Swan-Neck Hoes with 60-inch handles and either a 6- or 9-inch blade for $22.50 and $23.50. Smith and Hawkens' Stalham Hoe costs $28. A Diamond Scuffle Hoe from GSC goes for $22.50.

Finding Quality

Buying top-quality gardening tools isn't as easy as it should be. Likely places to find them are large, well-stocked hardware stores, garden-supply stores, and lawn-and-garden centers. Other sources are suppliers of industrial equipment, whom you can find in the Yellow Pages or by asking local contractors where they buy their industrial-grade tools. Study the catalogues of mail-order houses specializing in garden supplies, too, but if you buy by mail, be sure you can return any tool that doesn't fit you or feel right in your hands. Smith and Hawken, for example, offer a no-questions-asked guarantee on anything they sell.

Horticulture has a long and distinguished history in Europe, and it is therefore not surprising that many of the best gardening tools come from England and the Continent. There are some good American-made tools, too, but you have to know what they are and where to find them. Ames, True Temper, and Union Fork and Hoe are the three major manufacturers of garden tools in the United States. Their products come in three grades that follow the good-better-best scheme. The "Best" tools are for professional or contractor use. "Good" ones will serve the homeowner quite adequately for odd jobs around the place, but the fussy gardener who uses his or her tools a lot will want no less than "Better" and will probably be happiest with "Best." Another term you'll see is "Promotional," which designates everybody's poorest line, offered at prices competitive with those of cheap imports.

Tool grades are stamped into the handle. In True Temper's system, tools labeled "Professional" (five stars) are best. "Premium" (four stars) means better, and "Quality" (three stars) is good. Promotional tools are stamped with one star. Union Fork and Hoe grades are "Union Deluxe," "Union Standard," "Union," and, for the import busters, "Made in U.S.A." These seemingly transparent systems are of only limited use to the consumer for two reasons: (1) Advertising managers are sometimes too free with their use of "best" and "better." For example, True Temper's hollowback Dynalite shovels are marked with five stars. The designation is correct in the sense that the Dynalite line is the best of True Temper's hollowback tools, but I doubt that anyone at True Temper would argue that even the very best of hollowback shovels is as good as their solid-socket Fox shovels, which also carry five stars. (2) While all True Temper tools carry a grade designation, some Union Fork and Hoe lines carry product names only and are not graded "Deluxe," "Standard," or "Union." Ames identifies good, better, and best by product names only and has no immediately transparent grading system. So, to sum up, manufacturers' quality designations can be an aid to the consumer, but design remains the more dependable guide; if we use it as our major criterion, an overview of spades and shovels would look something like this:

	AMES	TRUE TEMPER	UNION FORK AND HOE
Best *(solid socket)*	Husky-Bronco Pony	Fox Bantam (both 5 star)	Union Deluxe
Very good *(closed back)*	Steel-Lite	Dynalite Powerback (5 star)	Razorback + 4 Jet-Lite

	AMES	TRUE TEMPER	UNION FORK AND HOE
Adequate *for most home use (hollow back)*	Peerless Ram	Dynalite (5 star)	Razorback
Border-line cases *(hollow back)*	dig ezy American Made	C-Series (4 star) S-Series (3 star)	Union Repeater Union Standard Union
Promotional *(hollow back)*	Eagle	Jim Dandy shovels (and other 1-star tools)	Made in U.S.A.

Just a couple of footnotes: Pony follows Husky-Bronco not because it is inferior but because it is uses a lighter, 15-gauge steel. Husky-Bronco has 14-gauge blades. (In steel, the lower the gauge number, the heavier the metal. Fourteen gauge is .0766 inch, 15 = .0689, 16 = .0613.) The same applies to True Temper's Fox and Bantam tools, and Union, too, offers lighter and heavier models in its solid-socket line. Similarly, the Razor-Back + 4 is the heaviest closed-back No. 2 round-point shovel on the market. Steel-Lite, Dynalite Powerback, and Jet-Lite are all lighter by about half a pound. In the hollowback tools, both weight and quality decline as you go down the columns. I could go on all night listing the fine points, but the important points remain very simple: (1) Pass up "Borderline" and "Promotional." (2) Select your tools from the "Best" and "Very Good" grades, or from "Adequate" if you will not be putting them to constant and demanding use. Remember, too, that no chart like this can do full justice to reality and that there may be specific tools in the "adequate" or even "borderline" categories that may suit a specific need. For example, the American companies make a line of so-called floral tools, which are smaller and lighter than standard-size tools. Ruggedness and durability will mean little to you if your tools are too big and heavy to use comfortably. Here too, however, the English fill the bill with their border forks and spades, which are small and light but also very well made.

The manufacturers' grading systems apply to all tools, not just digging tools. If you're looking at rakes or hoes, you'll find True Temper's stars or Union Fork and Hoe's "Deluxe," "Standard," or "Union" stamped on them, too. In Ames tools, the brand names listed above apply only to digging tools. For other tools, a blue stamp marks the better grades, a red one, the lower grades.

Manufacturers

AMES
Box 1774
Parkersburg, West Virginia 26101

TRUE TEMPER
P.O. Box 3500
Shiremanstown, Pennsylvania 17011

UNION FORK AND HOE
P.O. Box 1940
Columbus, Ohio 43216

Mail-order Houses

CLAPPER'S
1125 Washington Street
West Newton, Massachusetts 02165

GARDENER'S EDEN
P.O. Box 7307
San Francisco, California 94120

GARDENER'S SUPPLY CO.
128 Intevale Road
Burlington, Vermont 05401

A. M. LEONARD, INC.
6665 Spiker Road
Piqua, Ohio 45356

SMITH AND HAWKEN
25 Corte Madera
Mill Valley, California 94941

Fences for the Small Homestead

Fences are necessary evils we resort to for keeping some kind of creature in, some other kind of creature out, or both. That so many beautiful fences exist is a tribute to the human capacity to make the best of a bad situation.

The most beautiful and enduring fences—and the ones that rely least on technology and on the use of nonrenewable resources—are unfortunately the most costly in terms of time, labor, or money. No fence is more pleasing to the eye or more effective than a European hedgerow, but it takes years of work to grow one from scratch; and even after it has become dense enough to bar passage of man or beast, it still requires constant tending to keep new growth circling back into the hedgerow rather than reaching for the sky.

The next most attractive and durable alternative is a stone wall. Stone was the choice of early farmers in New England who made their pasture fences of loose stone cleared from their fields. Stone was also the choice of the indomitable Scott and Helen Nearing, who never shunned hard work or long-term projects and who built their concrete-and-stone garden wall a section and layer at a time using movable forms. If you collect the stone and do the building yourself, the cash outlay is minor, but the cost in time and labor can be daunting. It took the Nearings fourteen years of spare-time work to finish the 420 feet of wall around their garden in Maine.

Usually, the need for a fence is urgent. Your sheep are decimating your neighbor's strawberry field, or the deer are decimating your orchard. You either get a fence *right now* or forget sheep and orchards. And even if you should decide you want a hedgerow or a wall built for the ages, you may well need a temporary or semipermanent fence to tide you over until that one- or three- or ten-year project is completed.

In analyzing any fencing problem, you'll have to consider a number of factors. First is purpose. What is the most formidable adversary your fence will face? Dairy cows are probably the easiest animals to contain; then come beef cattle, horses, pigs, sheep, and goats. Even more difficult than keeping goats in is keeping predators out (and raccoons in a corn patch definitely rank as predators).

Aesthetics matter, too, particularly if you are fencing an area close to your house or one that you have to look at all the time in your daily comings and goings. What may be tolerable to the eye on the back forty may not be in the pasture next to your dooryard.

Is the terrain you want to fence reasonably flat, or is it hilly and shot through with ditches, gullies, and intermittent streams? Some fencing goes up hill and down dale easily; some does not.

Durability is desirable, provided your fence turns out to be just where you want it. A garden wall of stone is not such a good idea if you should decide, after it is built, that the garden should be moved to take advantage of better exposure or drainage. In his book *Building Fences of Wood, Stone, Metal, and Plants,* John Vivian suggests not only that you plan your fence carefully on paper but that you also lay it out on the ground with stakes and string and live with this practice fence for as long as it takes to assure yourself that the fence and any gates in it allow convenient movement of people, livestock, vehicles, and equipment. You may find yourself drastically altering your original plan or abandoning the idea of a fence in that location altogether. And even if you have run the string-and-stakes experiment, it may be a good idea—in critical locations particularly—to live with a temporary fence for a year before you build a permanent one.

Add cost to all these factors, and you should now be ready to sort out your priorities and decide what kind of fence—or what combination of fences—you want to use.

If, for example, you want to fence in a pasture that only horses will use, if the road or drive to your place borders that pasture and the appearance of the fence is important to you, and if cost is no object, the obvious choice is classic wooden horse fence—split rail, round rail, or post-and-board. Materials for any of them will probably run from $2.50 to $3 per running foot. A post-and-board fence is simple—but not easy—to build. Posts are typically 4-by-4s or 6-by-6s and 8 to 10 feet long, so they are not easy to handle. Also, they need to be set anywhere from 2½ to 4 feet into the ground, a task that calls for a tractor and auger if you have a large area to fence. Two to four rails are then nailed to the inside of the posts. The top one should be higher than your tallest horse's shoulder, and in the bottom three feet, rails should be spaced at least 14 inches apart and the lowest rail should be 14 inches from the ground so that a horse can easily extract a foot poked through the fence. Painted white, a post-and-board fence is a graceful addition to any farm. With some replacement of planking, it should be good for a quarter of a century.

But if economy takes precedence over beauty, the choice would be woven-wire or electric fence (or a combination of the two). Woven wire comes in a vast array of sizes, strengths, and configurations suitable for everything from cattle to poultry. It is the traditional sheep and goat fence because it is smooth, which prevents both injuries and snagging in wool. It is also dense and strong enough to prevent escape. The specifications are shown in catalogs and on tags in what looks like an arcane code, but it is easily cracked: 1047-6-12½ means that the fence has 10 horizontal strands, is 47 inches high, has 6-inch gaps between vertical stays, and is made of 12½-gauge wire. Where you see gauge given as

10/12½, the top and bottom wires are 10 gauge. Standard rolls are 20 rods (330 feet) long.

Square Deal horse fence has stays spaced only 2 inches apart to prevent hoof entrapment. This 12½-gauge fencing is available in 3-, 4-, 5-, and 6-foot heights. The 16-strand, 5-foot style costs about $90 for a 100-foot roll. Sheep fencing is usually of 12½-gauge wire, too, and stands 3 to 4 feet high. Horizontal strands can vary from 6 to 10 in those sizes. The more there are, the less the fence will yield to a phalanx of sheep plowing into it, and the extra dollars you'll pay for a 1047 fence ($98.99 for a 20-rod roll at my local Agway) instead of a 635 ($75.99) are probably worth it.

For goats, those most capricious and acrobatic of creatures, Red Brand poultry and rabbit fence (don't let the name put you off) is an excellent choice. This 14½-gauge fencing (the higher the number, the lighter the gauge) has a much denser weave than sheep fence. The 5-foot style, best suited for goats, has 23 horizontal wires and stays at 6-inch intervals. A 165-foot roll costs about $56. Then, to prevent goats from climbing, it's wise to add an electrified scare wire a foot off the ground and one on the top of the fence, too.

Poultry and rabbit fence is also available in a 6-foot height with 26 horizontal strands graduated at 1- to 4-inch intervals from bottom to top; price for 165 feet, about $65. This is a good choice for a large, permanent poultry yard. Traditional chicken wire in 2-inch mesh, being much lighter (20 gauge), is quick and easy to put up but is also prone to sagging, corroding, and tearing. For a family with only a dozen or so chickens, it makes more sense to fence in the garden and let the birds range free.

If you can supply your own posts or buy them cheaply, woven wire makes an economical fence, though its weight and stiffness make a tractor or four-wheel drive almost essential for installing it. Its great disadvantage is a tendency to sag and stretch under the weight of livestock and, in northern climes, of frost, thaws, and snows. That is doubly true of chicken wire. Then, too, for many uses, woven wire needs an assist from a strand or two or three of electric fencing, as for containing goats and fending off predators. And where 4- or 5-foot high chicken wire stapled to solid posts and extended down into the ground as an apron may keep rabbits and burrowing animals out of your garden, it will be useless against corn-raiding raccoons unless it is beefed up with an electric strand or two.

Both versatile and economical, the so-called New Zealand electric fencing systems deserve the careful attention of anyone who needs to upgrade an existing fence or install a new one. High-tensile wire for permanent boundary fences, which can be electrified or not, has the virtues of requiring fewer posts than traditional fencing, eliminating sag, lasting up to 60 years, and costing less than traditional permanent fencing. Polywire, a blend of stainless steel filaments braided together with polyethylene filaments, makes an easily constructed temporary or semipermanent fence, and electric netting (Premier calls theirs Electronet) provides perhaps the most dependable, effective, and easily moved fencing there is. Energizers can be run off household current, batteries, or solar panels.

Barbed wire is the one fence inappropriate for any use on the small homestead where you are dealing with only a few truly domestic animals. It can inflict painful and easily infected wounds on all livestock, slash horsehide to ribbons, snag sheeps' wool, and make hamburger of the belly and udder of any high-spirited goat that tries to climb or hurdle it.

More Information on Fencing

Detailed instructions for building a stone wall with movable forms are in Helen and Scott Nearings' *Living the Good Life* (New York: Schocken Books, 1970), Chapter 3: "We Build a Stone House."

John Vivian's *Building Fences of Wood, Stone, Metal, and Plants* (Charlotte, Vermont: Williamson Publishing Co., 1987) is perhaps the most comprehensive and detailed single volume available on fence building.

S. Chamberlin and J. Pollock, *Fences, Gates, and Walls: How To Design and Build* (Tucson, Arizona: HP Books, 1983) and *How To Build Fences and Gates,* Donald W. Vandervort, ed. (Menlo Park, California: Lane Books, 1971) both focus mainly on residential fencing but have many ideas and illustrations useful to the rural fence builder.

If you want to know how fencing was built in the nineteenth century, and still can be, read George A. Martin, *Fences, Gates, and Bridges: A Practical Manual,* originally published in 1887 and reprinted in 1974 by the Stephen Greene Press, Brattleboro, Vermont.

Two brief introductions to farm fencing—New Zealand fencing not included—are James FitzGerald, *The Best Fences,* Garden Way Publishing Bulletin A-92 (Pownal, Vermont: Storey Communications, Inc., 1984) and *Fences for the Farm and Rural Home,* USDA Farmers' Bulletin No. 2247, U.S. Government Printing Office, Washington, D.C. 20402, 1971.

Keystone Steel and Wire, makers of Square Deal horse fence and Red Brand woven-wire fencing, publishes a booklet that explains the basics of woven wire and lists all of Keystone's products. Free copies are available from Keystone at 7000 S.W. Adams Street, Peoria, Illinois 61641.

For a thorough and straightforward introduction to New Zealand fencing, send $4 to Premier Sheep Supplies Ltd., P.O. Box 89, Washington, Iowa 52353, for their manual *The New Fencing Systems Made Simple: A Do-It-Yourself Guide to Buying and Building Better Fences.*

High-Tensile Wire Fencing, published by the Northeast Regional Agricultural Engineering Service, 152 Riley Robb Hall, Ithaca, NY 14853, contains detailed instructions on building high-tensile fence, including a special section on designs for deer control.

Simple Machines

The science of physics as it's practiced these days is a pretty arcane business calling for fancy headwork and big, expensive machines like accelerators and cyclotrons and what-not. Fortunately, the physics you need around the homestead and woodlot requires little sophistication and not much more than the five elementary machines: the lever, the pulley, the inclined plane, the screw, and the wheel and axle. Of these, the first three are the primary machines; the last two are derivative and therefore secondary. The screw is just an inclined plane wound around a core; the wheel and axle constitute a rotary lever. Alone or hooked together in combinations, these elementary machines multiply our puny human powers so that we can move mountains, almost.

If any machine deserves the title of the machine primeval, it is the lever, a machine we use so much that we tend to take it for granted. When I stick the tip of my spade under a rock and pry it up out of the ground or when I twist the key on a can of sardines, I rarely think, "Ah, leverage, old friend! Thanks for this nice mechanical advantage." Even more rarely do I think what type of lever I'm using or, indeed, even that there are different types of levers. But there are. A Class 1 lever is the kind we probably all think of when we hear the word "lever," and it is probably the kind Archimedes had in mind when he said he could move the world with it if he just had some place to stand. It's also the kind we use when we pry the rock out of the garden with a spade. The fulcrum is placed *between* the operator and the weight to be lifted.

The mathematical formula describing the workings of this lever is so simple that even I can understand it. If the length of the effort arm (the distance from the operator to the fulcrum) is 5 feet and the length of the resistance arm (the distance from the fulcrum to the load to be moved) is 1 foot, then the mechanical advantage is 5, and with a little over 100 pounds of effort you can lift 500 pounds. The price you pay for that advantage is that you have to exert your effort over a much greater distance than the load will travel. The proportions are the same as your mechanical advantage. For every foot you move the load, your end of the lever will have to move 5 feet. But that, we all feel, is a cheap price to pay for the ability to move loads we otherwise could not move at all. And it is the underlying principle at work in almost all applications of simple machines: If we are willing to exert a relatively small force over a long distance, the machine will let us move a very heavy weight over a short distance.

In Class 2 levers, of which the wheelbarrow and the nutcracker are examples, the mathematics are the same, but the arrangement of the elements is different. The Class 2 lever puts the fulcrum at one end, the effort at the other, and the load somewhere in between. The distance from the handles of the wheelbarrow to its axle (the fulcrum) is the effort arm; the distance from the load to the fulcrum is the resistance arm. Here, too, the mechanical advantage is the ratio of effort arm to resistance arm. The longer, in other words, the wheelbarrow handles are and the closer to the wheel the load is, the less effort you will have to expend to lift that load.

We make levers out of different materials and give them special refinements of shape to make them perform specific tasks. Crowbars are made of steel and have points like a thick cold chisel so that they can pound into rocks without suffering undue harm. Wrecking bars have a curled claw that both grabs nail heads and provides its own fulcrum. In the woodlot, the lever is nearly as indispensable as the saw; and the lever best suited to lumbering is the peavey, a tool with a metal head that has a pike tip and, mounted on one side of it, a hook that swings free on a pivot. The hardwood handle is thick (anywhere from 2¼ to 2½ inches) where it fits into the ferrule and takes the most stress, but it then tapers down to a size more manageable for human hands.

The hook is the peavey's unusual feature, but even if you never made use of the hook, the peavey would still be, as a lever, far superior in the woods to just any straight, strong stick of the same length. You can easily drive a peavey in under a log of moderate size and toss the log to one side, first one end then the other—a much faster way of moving timber than rolling it. Where a blunt stick would not fit under the log or give you any purchase in the ground, the tapered head of the peavey drives in like a wedge, and the pike tip digs into the ground for a firm hold (Class 2 lever). These same features let you pry apart logs jammed together in a pile (Class 1), and the pike is small enough that you can use the tip of it to untie a tangle of logging chain. If I remember correctly, Paul Bunyan used a peavey as a toothpick.

The peavey has its uses in felling, too. A tree that is notched and sawn through but still doesn't want to go over can often be given the extra nudge it needs if you drive the peavey pike into the trunk as high as you can comfortably reach and then push the tree over. (The tree itself in this case is a nutcracker that has you outclassed until you can apply enough counterforce to open its jaws.) An even more powerful way of accomplishing this is to cut a pole about seven or eight feet long, set the tip of it up under a tree limb or into a notch you cut in the trunk, then use your peavey as a Class 2 lever against the butt of the pole, which then serves as a link to transfer the force of the lever to a point high up on the tree trunk. Still a third possibility is to drive a wedge (which is just a double inclined plane) into the saw kerf with a sledge hammer and tilt the tree on over that way.

Peaveys come in increments of 6 inches and range from 3 to 5½ feet. For someone my height (5 feet 8 inches) a 3½-foot one is about right—long enough to supply some leverage but not so long that it's ungainly. The pike tip adds a few inches to the tool's length, so a 3½-footer actually measures about 45 or 46 inches. If you're tall or if you're willing to sacrifice the handiness of a shorter tool for the increased leverage of a longer one, then get a longer handle.

But no matter how long a peavey you have, you'll no doubt run into situations where it is too short. What you do then is cut yourself as long a pole as you need and can manage and use that. A friend of mine told me recently how he extricated his pickup truck from a bog hole he drove into, thinking, mistakenly, that it was frozen over. He cut himself a long cedar pole and kept working his way around the truck, levering up one wheel after another while somebody else built up makeshift corduroy under the wheels. When he had a solid enough base, he drove out of the soup.

If the idea of picking up a truck with a stick sounds a little farfetched, just check it out with the figures. If he was lifting 1,000 pounds at each wheel (he was probably lifting less), and if the distance from the wheel to the fulcrum was one foot, then by exerting slightly over 100 pounds pressure on a lever measuring 10 feet from the fulcrum to him, he could raise the wheel ($1{,}000 \times 1 = 100 \times 10$). Always skeptical of mere numbers myself, I just went outside to run a hands-on test: I could easily lift the wheels of my Volkswagen Rabbit off the ground with a lousy little 8-foot 2-by-4. No sweat.

What the peavey has, however, that no stick from the woods can have, is the hook. By giving you a purchase on the side of a log, the hook lets you roll large, heavy logs that would otherwise be difficult, if not impossible, to move at all. You can saw halfway through a monster, then roll it over to finish your cuts from the other side. Log rolling is the hook's major function, but it by no means exhausts the peavey's bag of tricks. If you are less than precise in felling a tree and hang it up in another one, you can often free it by twisting it with the peavey. You can also use the peavey as a crude come-along by hooking a chain to the object you want to move, sticking the peavey hook into a chain link, catching the pike behind an immovable object or driving it into a tree stump, then pulling on the end of the handle. The peavey is also a godsend in building with logs, which requires endless rolling, prying, wiggling, and adjusting. Once you have some experience with a peavey, it makes moving logs almost (but not quite) as easy as tossing firewood billets around with your hands.

What the hook on the peavey does is create the rudimentary elements of a windlass or simple winch every time you roll a log. A windlass consists of a long handle attached to a drum on which a rope or cable is wound. The key on the sardine can is a miniature windlass that winds the can cover up on its axle. In terms of leverage, a windlass is just a Class 2 lever that keeps rotating around its fulcrum. It could also be described as a wheel with only one spoke, which you use as a rotary lever to overcome resistance on the drum. In the peavey "windlass," the resistance is in the weight of the log itself, not on the end of a rope, but the principle is the same. The tip of the peavey handle, with you applying some moderate force, describes a large arc; the log, a small one. The mechanical advantage is the ratio of the radius of the circle the peavey describes (again, the effort arm) to the radius of the log (the resistance arm).

The hand winch or, as it is more commonly known, the come-along, operates just the way the peavey and the log do, albeit in a much smaller, lighter, more sophisticated package. When you pull on the come-along handle, you wind a thin aircraft cable onto a small-diameter drum. When the lever reaches the end of its arc, a ratchet holds the drum in place, and you take the lever back to the start for another haul, just as you reset the peavey in the log for another roll. As long as we had nothing but bulky rope to work with, winches had to have large drums to accommodate it. But with the advent of steel cables ⅛- to ¼-inch thick and with rated breaking strengths of 2,000 to 4,200 pounds, it was possible to wind 25 feet of cable onto drums only a few inches in diameter and to build big mechanical advantages into small packages that weighed only 8 to 12 pounds. These miniwinches require only one reasonably strong arm to operate them, not four men leaning into capstan bars and singing a sea chanty. A 20-inch lever cranking a drum with a 2-inch radius, for example, gives you a mechanical advantage of 10. Discounting friction, you can lift 1,000 pounds with a little over 100 pounds of effort.

The come-alongs you'll find in your local hardware store usually appear in two versions. The first is the basic hand winch, which simply winds cable onto a drum. The mechanical advantage, which is usually somewhere between 12 and 15, is provided solely by the winch. The second version incorporates a pulley, still another simple machine, into the cable. What a single pulley does, if it is attached to the load to be moved, is cut the required force in half, thus doubling the mechanical advantage. So, if you needed a 100-pound pull on the handle of the basic winch to move 3,000 pounds, the addition of the pulley will let you move that same load with a 50-pound effort. The hitch is, of course, in accordance with the old lesser-effort-longer-distance rule, that the pulley will oblige you to wind 12 feet of cable onto the winch drum to move the load 6 feet.

This trade-off makes clear why pulleys are of somewhat limited use and why the hand winch has become the simple machine of preference for so many lifting and hauling chores. A basic block-and-tackle has two double blocks in it, that is, each block contains two revolving sheaves. Where a single pulley yields a mechanical advantage of two, this system yields one of four. Each strand of rope or "fall" that runs through the movable block bears its proportion of the load, so the mechanical advantage is equal to the number of falls. But for each fall you add, you also need a longer and longer and still longer pull to operate the system.

To lift 600 pounds 5 feet with a single pulley (two falls), you need a 300-pound effort exerted through 10 feet. To accomplish the same work with a double block (four falls) takes 150 pounds of effort and 20 feet of rope pulled through the machine. A triple block and six falls equal 100 pounds and 30 feet of rope. To duplicate the mechanical advantage of the hand winch would require a hugely cumbersome system of blocks and miles of rope in which to tangle oneself. Also, the more blocks you use, the greater the friction in the system becomes, and the more effort has to go into operating it.

But don't toss out that old block and tackle you have hanging in the barn. If you are handling loads within its capabilities, it has a couple of great advantages over the hand winch: speed and ease of adjustment. A come-along moves at a snail's pace, a few inches per haul. The speed of operation for a block and tackle is limited only by how fast you can run or pull, and because the operating load is usually kept fairly light, you can easily pull some rope in, let a little out, and fiddle to your heart's content. These are the reasons why booms on small sailboats are controlled by simple pulley systems. If a huge gust comes along, you have to be able to let the mainsail run out quickly; and if you're pointing up into the wind, you want to be able to fine-tune the set of your sail, taking in a few inches now, letting out a few later.

The other reason why it's worthwhile keeping some pulleys around even if you have a come-along is the same reason why one version of the cheap come-along has a pulley built into it: Combining pulleys with the hand winch lets you multiply the powers of the winch enormously. Lug-All, the manufacturer of high-quality, industrial come-alongs, sensibly builds its machines to be convertible from a straight hand winch to hand winch plus single pulley.

With a single pulley, as mentioned above, you double the capacity of a straight winch. Rigging that same winch with a four-fall block and tackle would quadruple its capacity, letting a come-along rated at 1,000 pounds move 4,000. But with all this macho, strong-arm talk about multiplying powers, keep an essential point of safety in mind: While simple machines bring the effort you have to exert down within your capabilities, the system in which that machine functions is still bearing the entire brunt of the load and has to be strong enough to handle it. Picture the example of the four-fall block and tackle hoisting 4,000 pounds with a come-along hitched to the floor doing the work. The come-along's load will be something over 1,000 pounds, that is, one-fourth of the load plus whatever it takes to overcome friction. But before you blithely start cranking those 4,000 pounds up into the air (it's a real cinch, right?) remember that the top block and the beam it is attached to have to sustain considerably more than 5,000 pounds—the weight of the load plus your downhaul. If they can't take it, there'll be a great crash. My local physics professor recommends a support system capable of handling twice the sum of the forces you will put on it.

If the come-along itself is in the direct line of pull, the machine is still bearing the full weight of the load, no matter how easy it may make it for you to move the load. Come-alongs are built to sustain heavier loads than their rated capacities. The inexpensive Maasdam Pow'r-Pulls, for example, claim a safety factor of 2:1, which means that a machine rated at a 1-ton capacity will presumably take up to a 2-ton load before it breaks, but I wouldn't push my luck. Also, because come-alongs have relatively short cable lengths, you will inevitably have to use them in connection with ropes or chains or both, and those components should be rated well above any loads you anticipate putting on them. The safe working loads of ropes vary with their construction and are usually only about 10 to 20 percent of the breaking strength, so for use with a 1-ton come-along, you should have a rope with a breaking strength of between 5 and 8 tons. A 3-strand, filament polyester rope in the ⅝- to ⅞-inch range would probably be about right. Nylon rope, while stronger per unit weight, is a poor choice for lifting and hauling because of its high elasticity. You use up half your come-along cable just stretching the rope, and a stretched rope is like a stretched rubber band. If it does break, its elasticity makes it act like a released slingshot. Any system under tension is potentially dangerous, of course. A chunk of broken hardware slung with the accumulated energy of a stretched rope is as lethal as shrapnel, so it behooves anyone using ropes, chains, and come-alongs to be extremely conservative in their use. Lug-All, conscious of the human capacity for error, builds extra safety factors into their come-alongs. The handles will bend at 50 percent above the machine's rated load, and the hooks are made so that they will straighten out, not break, if they are overstressed.

A safety precaution you can take with any rope or cable under tension is to throw an old rug, heavy blanket, tarp, or whatever over it. If the line breaks, the heavy cloth will absorb and dampen the energy in it.

Safely used, simple machines lighten your work and make potentially onerous chores downright enjoyable. One of our fall rituals is hauling out the swimming dock we use all summer, a job that has us using every simple machine except a screw. To slide the dock up the steep bank, we set a couple of skids up as a primitive inclined plane. Then with a single pulley and a come-along, we haul the dock up over the steep bank. Once it is ashore, we make use of Class 1 levers to raise it up and slide a couple of rollers under it. Because the rollers ease the task so much, we can take the pulley out of the system and crank the dock the rest of the way to its wintering grounds with the come-along alone. I won't say it's no work, but it's a lot less work and a lot more fun that it would be without the lever, the pulley, the wheel, and the inclined plane.

Sources

As one would expect, the Peavey Manufacturing Company, P.O. Box 129, East Eddington, Maine 04428, offers the greatest variety of peaveys and related logging tools. You'll find the standard peavey in 3- to 5-foot lengths, all about $25; the Bangor or Rafting Peavey, which has its steel socket and pick forged together in one piece; pickeroons; hookeroons; pulp hooks; and pick poles. A note on nomenclature is perhaps in order: The peavey is named for Joseph Peavey, the Maine blacksmith who is credited with improving the design of the traditional cant dog, which had its hook mounted on a U-bolt. The U- bolt let the hook flop around uncontrollably, and the hook went where you wanted it to only if gravity was on your side. Peavey's design lets the hook move up and down only, not every which way, and so enables the user to aim it where he wants whether the tool is rightside up or upside down.

The term "cant dog" is still used today as a synonym for peavey.

A "cant hook," however, is a different tool. Instead of the pike tip of the peavey (or cant dog), it has a small hook on a blunt tip. This provides a firmer bite for rolling logs, but limits the usefulness of the cant hook for prying, poking, pushing, and jabbing into wood for a hold. For versatility in the woods, the peavey is the better tool.

For anyone operating a small sawmill, a short version of the cant hook called the Roll-On cant hook, available in 2- and 2½-foot lengths, is ideal for handling logs on the saw carriage. It is also a boon for anyone building with logs. Still another variation is the Peavey Company's Timber Jack, a cant hook with a triangular brace on the side opposite the hook. The brace holds a tree well up off the ground so that you can saw it, hew it, or peel it without risk of dulling your saw or axe. Other makers and suppliers of peaveys are the Snow and Nealley Company, P.O. Box 876, Bangor, Maine 04401, and Forestry Suppliers, Inc., P.O. Box 8397, Jackson, Mississippi 39204-0397.

For the high-quality of come-alongs, go to the Lug-All Corporation, Haverford, Pennsylvania 19041. Lug-All's machines cost significantly more than the hardware-store variety, but you get an industrial-grade tool that can stand up to years of daily use. Prices range from about $84 for a basic ½-ton model to $106 for a 1½-ton to $320 for a 3-ton. If you want special hooks or a marine-grade winch made of completely corrosion-resistant materials or any of Lug-All's other options, the prices will be higher. If you need durability, reliability, and an extra margin of safety in a winch you'll be putting to frequent use, the extra dollars for a Lug-All will be well spent.

If you need a come-along only for an occasional odd job, you'll probably be well enough satisfied with cheaper makes. The Maasdam 1-ton model 144 S-6 sells for about $30. The slightly heavier 144 SB-6, which uses a pulley to boost its capacity to two tons, retails for about $40. Because cheaper winches don't have the Lug-All's safety features, use them conservatively and inspect them frequently to be sure that all parts are in sound working order.

Carts and Barrows

Very high on my list of favorite wheelbarrow personages is sweet Molly Malone of Dublin, who, as you may recall, wheeled her wheelbarrow through the streets broad and narrow, crying, "Cockles and mussels, alive, alive-o." I've always wondered exactly what kind of wheelbarrow Molly wheeled. Was it what we usually mean when we say "wheelbarrow" these days, a one-wheeler with legs and handles in back, and did Molly have to lift half her load when she wanted to move down the streets broad and narrow? Or was it more a cart, as well it might have been, for English usage does not limit "wheelbarrow" exclusively to one-wheeled vehicles. I hope, for Molly's sake, that it was a pushcart something like the one street vendors in New York use for hawking orange juice and pretzels, a high, two-wheeled rig in which the load was balanced over the axle, so that all Molly had to do to move her cockles and mussels along was tilt the legs of her cart up off the street and walk ahead to the next corner.

The physics of a well-designed cart—whether for hawking or gardening—are such that 5 pounds of lift exerted on the handle and not much more in the way of push or pull will let you scoot

400-pound loads around. A cart with the load evenly distributed on either side of the axle is like a see-saw with two kids of more or less equal weight on either end. That is the cart's virtue, but it is also one of its vices, for if one kid jumps off the see-saw, the other hits the deck. And if you unload the back of your cart before you unload the front, you may get a mouthful of handle.

The cart I have in mind here is the classic spoke-wheeled, plywood-bodied, metal-trimmed garden cart. I almost called it the Garden Way cart, because that's the one I've had for years, and though there are many companies now that make carts of this kind, the Garden Way remains the prototype and granddaddy of them all. As I've just suggested, the greatest favor a cart does for you is put the load on the cart's axle and wheels. A wheelbarrow, by contrast, divides the load between its front wheel and your back, arms, and shoulders. The farther forward the load is on the barrow and the longer the handles are, the more the wheel carries and the less you carry. But there are practical limits to handle length, and you always wind up carrying quite a lot.

None of this is to say that a wheelbarrow is inferior to a cart. It's just different, and anybody who has a variety of trundling chores to take care of will probably want both. If we press the comparison a little further, it's easy to see why. Because the cart takes the load off you and on itself, it can be much larger and carry much more than a wheelbarrow. With its two wheels instead of one, a cart is laterally stable. You can pile on twice its height with hay or apple-tree prunings, and unless you ride one wheel up on a rock or drop it into a ditch, you won't lose your load. The large wheels ride up and over minor obstacles, and two wheels are more maneuverable and create less friction than four.

I used to move my firewood from outdoor drying shed to the wood room in my ell with my tractor and farm trailer until I discovered how much more efficient the Garden Way cart was. True, the trailer took much larger loads, but because I can place the cart within inches of where I'm actually working, I save both time and strength that used to go into tossing wood onto the trailer and carting armfuls of it from the trailer to its final destination. The cart is big enough to take a respectable load but small enough to put it right where I want it.

But please note that the lay of the land here is ideal for carting heavy loads. The terrain is flat and the ground firm. The open-sided drying shed and the garage doors of the woodroom leave plenty of space for maneuvering the cart. If you had to move those same heavy loads of rock maple and yellow birch up or down a hill, the cart would work against you. If you tilt downhill, the cart goes nose-heavy, its handle pulls your arms up in the air, and it can start to run away with you. Because it weighs much more than you do, it takes some fancy and energetic heel work to put on the brakes. Going uphill, you are equally outweighed. The handle bar wants to drop down to your knees, and even if you have the muscle to moose the cart uphill, you may not have the traction, and your feet will spin like bald tires on ice. It will improve your traction and purchase to pull the cart when going uphill, and some people prefer pulling to pushing on any terrain because it is easier to pull the wheels over small obstacles than it is to push them.

Because moving my firewood from drying shed to woodroom involves no hills (or rocks or potholes that will hang up the wheels of a heavily laden cart), the cart is the conveyance of choice. A wheelbarrow's smaller carrying capacity would oblige me to make two or three times as many trips back and forth. To compensate for that, I would no doubt pile the wheelbarrow too high and make it so heavy and top heavy that I would (a) get tired very fast, (b) tip the damn thing over, and (c) hurt my toe when I kicked it.

There are circumstances, however, in which one would kick the cart and praise the wheelbarrow. At one point in my history, as chore boy at a fishing camp in northern Maine, I was responsible for keeping the wood box in the lodge kitchen filled. The route from the woodshed led down a short but steep hill, passed through a narrow defile between two large rocks and almost as narrow an alleyway between the ice house and the lodge, went through the kitchen door, skirted kitchen table and cupboards, and ended at the woodbox. Maneuverability, not carrying capacity, was of the essence here, and I used an old-fashioned wooden wheelbarrow with its sides removed. A cart wouldn't have fit through any of the slots I had to pass, and for negotiating hills, the weight that the wheelbarrow puts onto you is an advantage. It increases your traction either for braking on a downslope or pushing on an uphill.

With those principles established—carts for big, bulky, and heavy loads on level terrain, wheelbarrows for smaller loads on narrow, tortuous, hilly routes—we can consider some finer points of cart and barrow design and see how they ease or complicate different chores.

A standard Garden Way cart with a vertical, nonremovable front panel is misery to dump. I am reminded of that fact every fall when I try to empty the cart of leaves, cornstalks, or other compostables. The only way you can really clear it is to flip it upside down and then pull it toward you a bit so that the front panel doesn't pick up some of your dumped load when you right the cart—an awkward and maddening business. Garden Way and other manufacturers have offered a remedy for this shortcoming: a removable front panel.

The cart's square snout, which makes it hard to dump, is not all bad, however. Indeed, it's a positive virtue when you want to pick up large rocks or other heavy objects that you could otherwise not load without the aid of an inclined plane. For tasks like that, the cart can function like a hand truck. You tip it up on its nose, roll the rock onto the front panel, then pull down on the handle. Assuming that the rock is not so heavy it tears the front panel right out of your cart, you're ready to roll.

In the loading and dumping department, the wheelbarrow's plus is, once again, the cart's minus, and vice-versa. The only way to load a wheelbarrow is the hard way: You just plain have to pick up the load and put it in the barrow. Conversely, any wheelbarrow—whether it is a contractor's metal-trayed job or the traditional wooden, garden barrow with removable sides—is a cinch to dump.

The primary mission of the contractor's barrow is to carry shifty or sloppy loads and to dump them right where you want them. I can't imagine using anything else to cart wet cement along a narrow, plank walkway and then, at the end of the walkway, to dump the load cleanly into a form eight inches wide. The front of the tray is sloped and curved to ease and direct the dump. The barrow handles extend beyond the wheel in front, and a metal crosspiece bolted across them acts as a shoe that stops the barrow and holds it firmly in place when you roll it up to dump it.

The garden wheelbarrow is designed to dump to the side, not the front. It has (or certainly should have) removable sides. All you do is pull the left or right panel and lay the barrow over on its side. The lack of the shoe in front of the wheel also makes it clear that this barrow is not meant to be dumped to the front. If you do tip it up on its nose, you can't hold it still. The removable sides on the garden barrow not only let it serve as a firewood carrier but also, with only one side removed, make it an ideal rolling workbench for carting seedlings into the garden and carrying your hand tools, watering can, or whatever up and down the rows with you.

The classic garden barrow has some other features, too, that are better adapted to the garden than they are to the building site. The sides fit into brackets on the handles and are no wider than the handles themselves. The resulting body, which is narrow and deep rather than wide and shallow and which usually has a capacity of three and a half to four cubic feet, has two advantages: It is easy to balance, and it passes more easily between rows in the garden. The wide, bowl-like tray of the contractor barrow is fine for dumping loose materials, but because the tray extends beyond the handles, it makes this kind of wheelbarrow much harder to balance, as anyone knows who has felt the irregularities of garden terrain flip a loaded contractor barrow out of his or her grip. I have even had the misfortune, on soft soil, of driving the front shoe of a contractor barrow into the ground and piling headlong into the back of the barrow—an exercise that is hard on the belly and shins.

A classic garden barrow also has a large-diameter wooden wheel with a narrow rim and a steel tire. Like the narrow-rimmed wheels on a racing bicycle, this type of wheel reduces friction to a minimum and has the additional advantage of never going flat or wearing out. Appropriate as this hard, narrow wheel is for a garden wheelbarrow, it is just the wrong thing for a contractor's barrow. There, the wide, pneumatic tire provides added traction when you get up on those narrow plank catwalks; it damps the vibration you would get from running a hard wheel on pavement, and it absorbs the shock that you would otherwise absorb in your arms and shoulders whenever you run a heavily laden barrow into even a minor obstacle on the ground. And a contractor's barrow is, almost by definition, heavily laden. The most common size (5¾ cubic feet) tallies out to about 450 pounds of wet concrete.

Each of these conveyances—cart, garden wheelbarrow, and contractor wheelbarrow—is job specific, and which ones you choose will depend on what it is you have to do. William Carlos Williams was pretty clear about his choice in this matter. He wrote:

So much
depends
upon
a red wheel
barrow
glazed with rain
water
beside the white
chickens.

I can see the very wheelbarrow he meant. It's the classic red wheelbarrow, one with a wooden-spoked and wooden-rimmed wheel and maybe even with some discreet trim or design stenciled on its sides. Much does depend on it, both in a practical and poetic sense, and it deserves all the honor Williams has heaped upon it. But if I'm faced with a gravel pile or woodpile, I'll not scorn the homelier metal-bellied barrow or the plywood cart with its bicycle wheels either.

Choosing Carts and Barrows

The Garden Way cart (and its imitators) comes in two sizes. I prefer the larger one (about $170 from Garden Way, Inc., 102d Street and 9th Avenue, Troy, New York 12180, 800-828-5500) not only because of its greater carrying capacity (13½ cubic feet and a 400-pound maximum load versus 6½ cubic feet and a 300-pound maximum load in the medium model) but also because the 26-inch wheels keep the cart body higher off the ground than do the 20-inch wheels of the smaller model, making the cart less snag prone on the rough terrain I frequent.

Then, too, the leg design on the larger cart keeps the loops in the legs parallel to the direction of travel rather than across it. Legs of that kind are snag proof, do not bang into your shins, and won't poke you in the belly if you tip the cart forward.

The essential points of a practical cart are large wheels and a large, flat-bed body. I would avoid like the plague those ubiquitous V-shaped "garden carts" with dinky little 10-inch plastic wheels. They hang up on the smallest mole hill and oblige you to claw and scratch around in the bottom of the V to empty them.

In metal-bodied wheelbarrows, I would pass up the "homeowner" grades and stick with the industrial and contractor grade, which means a tire no less than 16 inches in diameter and a tray of no less than 4½ cubic-foot capacity. Ames, True Temper, and Union Fork and Hoe all offer a number of wheelbarrows of this kind from about $90 to $125. An option in the large (5¾ cubic-foot) barrows is a polyethylene tray instead of a metal one. This takes about 6 to 10 pounds off the barrow. I've never used a polyethylene tray and can't say how well it holds up.

The J. K. Adams Company of Dorset, Vermont, makes a very handsome and sturdy gardener's wheelbarrow. The spoked front wheel is a generous 20 inches in diameter; the frame is of oak with mortise-and-tenon joints. The color? Red. It's just what William Carlos Williams had in mind. The price is high ($225 from Clapper's, 1125 Washington Street, West Newton, Massachusetts 02165), but it should last a lifetime and never fail to delight both hand and eye.

THE WELL-DRESSED RUSTIC

Wool for Winter

It would be unfair to say that wool has been getting bad press these days, but its virtues have generally been neglected in all the hoopla about new miracle fabrics like PolarPuff and FiberFluff that are supposed to be so much better. Synthetic piles and fleeces have some laudable qualities, foremost among them their refusal to absorb water and the speed with which they dry; and there are uses for which even as conservative a curmudgeon as I will choose them.

But for all that, wool—wool pants, wool shirts and jackets, wool mitts, wool hats, wool socks—remains the heart of my cold-weather wardrobe. In *The Complete Walker III,* Colin Fletcher discusses the "quality of warmth" in both synthetic and natural fabrics, and he notes that "'plastic warmth' rarely if ever seems to move beyond a mere absence of coldness, while 'old-fashioned warmth' can and commonly does become a positive, glowing radiance—a luxurious sense of well-being, a sensual pleasure." Needless to say, clothing preferences are highly subjective; but my own metabolism and experience lead me to a more extreme statement: Where a pile jacket often leaves me vaguely chilly, a good wool jac shirt keeps me warm and comfortable.

In selecting woolen clothing, you'll want to consider quality, weight and type of fabric, and price. Wool comes in a horrendous number of grades that are determined by the breed of sheep, where it lives, what it eats, and even from where on the beast a particular handful happens to come. The customer in a store cannot determine any of these factors even if he or she wanted to, and unless you have enough experience to be able to tell just what you want by its look and feel, your best guarantee of getting a good product is to buy from a reputable retailer, like L. L. Bean, or to buy a name brand: Filson, Pendleton, Woolrich. Those are nationally known names, but you may also find excellent regional manufacturers. An example is Johnson Woolen Mills in Vermont whose primary market areas are the Northeast and upper Midwest.

The Woolmark, a symbol on a label sewn into a garment, identifies a product made of 100-percent new wool, that is, wool that has not been spun or woven prior to its use in that garment. The Woolblend mark identifies a fabric of no less than 60 percent wool blended with another fiber for durability. A very serviceable blend of this kind is the 85 percent wool, 15 percent nylon used in many Woolrich shirts.

The secret of happy wool wear is having a range of garments from light to heavy that can be layered for different conditions. "Innerwear" and "outerwear" become relative terms, for the wool shirt that is today's outer layer may well be tomorrow's inner layer if the temperature drops dramatically. A soft wool or wool-and-nylon blend of 8 to 10 ounces makes an ideal first layer. (Unless otherwise specified, the weight is per running yard of a 60-inch bolt.) In this category is Bean's Hunter Shirt ($33)—Ernest Hemingway was particularly fond of the black-and-white checked one—and Woolrich and Pendleton offer comparable shirts. The Pendletons, retailing at about $50, have a superb quality of wool and a nicety of tailoring that makes them particularly comfortable first-layer shirts over which a second layer slips without lumps or bulges. The Woolriches ($40) have a slightly "beefier" feel. You can't go wrong with either one.

The fabric in medium-weight shirts tips the scales at 13 to 16 ounces and is a thicker, air-trapping material that provides a lot of insulation. A typical pattern in this weight shirt is the big buffalo plaid; and Woolrich, logically enough, calls its 13- to 14-ounce line Buffalo shirts (about $40). Bean's comparable Maine Guide Shirt is slightly heavier at 16 ounces and sells for $33.

Layers one and two are often quite enough to see me through most New England winter weather, but if things get really mean, the next line of defense is a jac shirt in an 18- or 20-ounce fabric. As its name suggests, a jac shirt is somewhere between a shirt and a jacket. If you want one you can tuck into your pants, choose one with long tails and buttons. If you'll be wearing it more as a jacket, you may want a model with a square bottom and a zipper. A fabric often used in both styles is a diagonal twill that is not only warm but also tightly woven enough to provide some wind protection. All the major manufacturers of woolens offer jac shirts in a variety of models and colors and at prices from about $35 to $50.

If you want the ultimate in heavyweight wool, turn to the C. C. Filson Company of Seattle, Washington. Filson's prices are high ($83.50 for a jac shirt in 18-ounce wool, $137 for the famous Filson Mackinaw Cruiser in 26-ounce mackinaw cloth), but you'll get your money's worth in the exceptionally long life of the garment.

In pants, there are several classics to choose from. Among the winter favorites for old-time woodsmen are solid green pants in a 24-ounce blend of 80 percent wool and 20 percent nylon that are so closely associated with Johnson Woolen Mills of Johnson, Vermont, that they are known as "Johnson pants." Johnson also makes a heavier model (30 ounces) in gray with a red and green stripe overlay. These pants are tightly woven and then processed to give them a felt-like quality that makes them extremely wind resistant. At about $35 and $45 respectively, the green and gray Johnson pants are excellent buys.

For very vigorous activity, such as cross-country skiing, these heavy pants are too warm except for the bitterest of weather, and I find the pants I wear most often in the winter (not to mention the spring and fall) are Bean's Bird Shooting Pants, which are made of a tough 10-ounce (per square yard) wool whipcord that is both warm and wind-resistant. Their great versatility and comfort make them worth the price of $69.

On the subject of price, I should point out that with some careful shopping you won't always have to pay the list prices I've been quoting here. If you buy in high-volume, low-service outlets, you will pay about 25 percent less even in season; and in the spring and summer, clothing stores in my area mark winter woolens down 25 to 30 percent. Still another source of bargains is the army surplus store. All-wool U.S. Army dress green pants, for example, which make a much cheaper alternative to Bean's Bird Shooting Pants, routinely sell for $8. Surplus stores will often carry not only U.S. military clothing but also some first-rate woolens made for the military in Germany or Scandinavia. I've not had much luck finding suitable wool shirts at surplus stores (for some reason armies don't seem to believe in long shirttails), but there are good buys in pants, watch caps, and scarves.

Treats for the Hands and Feet

Ragg Socks

"Ragg" is Norwegian for "rough hair." A friend in the outfitting business tells me that the rough hair originally came from Norwegian goats and was blended with wool to make the characteristic mottled gray ragg yarn. The ragg socks you can buy now are usually a blend of 85 percent wool and 15 percent nylon minus the goat hair, but they still do a great job of keeping your feet warm. The smooth fit of the ones with stretch nylon is a great plus if you're wearing two or three layers of socks. I like Wigwam's 10-inch "Expedition" ones ($7.50).

Snowshoe Moccasins

The great curse of most modern cold-weather footgear is that it does not breathe enough to let foot perspiration escape. The result is a soggy, cold foot. Native American peoples have always understood that, and their cold-weather footwear still remains the best. Wear soft-leather moccasins over two pairs of ragg socks and a felt liner, and know what real deep winter comfort is. Remember, however, that these moccasins work only in cold, dry snow. In damp snow they quickly soak through. Depending on conditions, you will probably need to change to a rubber boot at temperatures above 15° Fahrenheit.

Buy a pair of felt liners that will fit comfortably over two pairs of heavy wool socks. The best liners I have found so far are the 3⁄8-inch thick Sorel liners, made by Kaufman Footwear of Kitchener, Ontario. They are 75 percent wool, 25 percent acetate, and have taped seams that improve durability. Price: around $12.

Mittens

For the hands it is hard to beat Austrian-made Dachstein mitts, which can be worn either alone or under a windproof shell as needed. These tightly woven, preshrunk mitts come in three weights. The heaviest is marked "Art. No. 16." Available from mountaineering and outfitting shops and by mail from Recreational Equipment, Inc. (REI) and others. About $14.

Hats for the Heat

What we human beings choose to wear on our heads is not governed solely by rational criteria. There is no practical reason why an archbishop should wear a mitre or a Sioux chieftain a great crown and train of eagle feathers or a four-star general a brass hat. The prime function of such headgear is not to keep off the sun or rain but to advertise the wearer's powers and authority, be they spiritual, physical, political, military, or all of the above.

The hat, however utilitarian it was to begin with, inevitably evolves into a symbol; and when it comes time for any of us to select a hat, we will probably give more weight to the mystique of our headgear than to its practicality. The people who sell hats know that. They also know that very few of us are—or even want to be—archbishops or four-star generals, so what we in fact find in the stores and catalogs are hats emanating mystiques that many more of us can reverberate to—an Indiana Jones, a Professional Hunter, an Open Road, a Snowy River, a Ghurka Hat.

But putting mystique aside for the moment, what exactly do we ask of a hat for haying or boating in the blazing sun of July, and what features will meet those needs? The mission is pretty straightforward. We want to shade our eyes and put a mini-roof and a layer of insulation between the top of our heads and the hammer blows of the sun. Ventilation is certainly desirable, and so is a light color that reflects heat rather than absorbing it. Light weight is another desirable feature, and to that the backpacker will add crushability.

Some hat designs will accomplish only part of the mission, but if that is the part you care most about, then well and good. The baseball cap and all its variations, ranging from your everyday adjustable mesh-sided job on up to L. L. Bean's Saltwater Sports Cap ($8) with its larger visor, are primarily eye shades and only secondarily protection from the sun. The traditional dark green underbrim reduces glare (a feature as useful to the boater as it is to the baseball player because most of the glare experienced on the water is reflected up from the surface). Fitting snugly on the head, however, the baseball cap leaves no insulating air space between the top of your head and the crown of the cap and it leaves the back of the neck exposed.

The French Foreign Legion kepi is still a cap but offers some hot-weather advantages over the baseball cap. The higher, cylindrical body creates some insulating air space, and a shoulder-length cloth flap in back protects the neck. The JanSport Desert Hat is a white, crushable model (with chin strap) made of 100 percent cotton ($6.99 from Campmor). Another popular variation on the billed cap is the Orvis Fishing Hat (Item No. 4674-26, $12.50), which adds to the large, wide visor a flap in back that can be worn turned up or pulled down to protect the back of the neck. Many fisherfolk favor green over white in this cloth hat, accepting the minor penalty of more heat absorption for the reduction in glare.

At the opposite end of the scale from the cap in size and perhaps the next best thing to sitting under a shade tree is the sombrero. *Sombra* means "shade" in Spanish, so a sombrero is quite literally a shade-maker. With a brim sometimes as wide as two feet, a sombrero can make a skinny man look like a walking beach umbrella. It's hardly the hat you'll roll up and stuff in your pack or back pocket, but it sure will keep the sun off your face and neck. The Spanish and Mexican aristocracy made their sombreros out of felt; the peasants used straw. Chalk up another win for the common man, at least in the summertime. The straw hats are lighter; they let whatever breezes there are blow through; and, of course, they are much cheaper. The cowboy hat, which is the sombrero's American cousin, comes in both felt and straw, too; and straw is as much the material of choice for hot, dry summer months in Arizona or Wyoming as it is in Mexico. Stetson and Resistol are the major makers of western hats, most of their straws running in the $40 to $75 range; the felts, from about $65 to $150. These hats as well as a vast offering of other hats from all over the world are available from Worth and Worth, Ltd., in New York City.

Straws come in a great variety of styles, colors, and textures. Depending on the fiber and finish of straws, their prices can range from about $250 for the Monte Cristi Panama Fedora, which Worth and Worth call "the rarest and most elegant straw hat in the world," down to 99 cents each for unfinished straw hats I found recently in a discount store.

"Unfinished" means that these hats consisted of raw, woven fiber with perhaps one row of stitching around the brim to keep the strands from unraveling. Some were made of hemp cord, others of a flattened grass stem, species undetermined. Ninety-nine cents isn't a bad price for the shade, ventilation, and light weight of a straw; but I'm willing to spend a little more to add a sweatband that keeps the woven straw from leaving a waffle pattern on my brow, the pressing that gives the hat a permanent shape, and the sizing that keeps the straw from constantly cracking, breaking, and crumbling away.

L. L. Bean has a line of "sea straw" hats that take their shapes from hats traditionally made of other materials: the Outback, an Australian stockman's pattern ($12.50); the Gambler, a familiar item in many a Western ($12.50); and the Pith Helmet ($13). The Pith Helmet has a headband adjustable to any size head. Woven of sea straw, this helmet allows even more air circulation than the old pith helmet. Sea straw, also called "sea grass," is hemp, but its various grades can produce hats that differ greatly from each other in appearance and feel. Another moderately priced hat of this type with a 2½-inch brim is the Seagrass Eagle Safari Hat ($13) from REI.

Perhaps the classiest of straws is the Panama hat, but don't let the image of a white Panama atop the head of a white-suited, cigarillo-smoking young blade in Rio make you think the Panama is just for the natty urban types. On the contrary, the genuine Panama, which is woven in Ecuador from fibers of the hat palm, makes an excellent summer hat for the outdoorsman or woman, hence the presence of broad-brimmed Panamas in gardening and sportswear catalogs as well as on the shelves of city haberdashers. The Panama is flexible and durable. Not only can it be rolled or folded for stowing away, but it can also be steamed and shaped to suit your fancy. Orvis and Smith and Hawken have broad-brimmed Panamas; Bean's has one with a slightly narrower brim; all run about $19.

The variety of materials and designs in lightweight cloth hats could fill a small phone book. The basic pattern is a fairly high crown (to lift the sun off your head) and a brim of about 2 or 2¼ inches. Subtleties of cut and stitching, the type and placement of ventilating grommets, and a rounded or flat top will yield everything from a Pork Pie to a Bush Hat to a New Zealand Potae. Because these hats are light in weight, eminently crushable, and compact when crushed, they make excellent backpacking and traveling hats. Cotton canvas is a cheap, cool, rugged material used in REI's Bush Hat ($5.95) and Crusher Hat ($8.95). The Bush Hat is a soft, flat-topped model; the Crusher, domed and with a green underbrim. Panache and detail work can add quite a bit more to the price of a canvas hat. The heavier cloth and more stylish cut of the REI Canvas Aussie Hat run its price up to $19.50. The Tilley T3 is a polyester/cotton blend, but its hand workmanship, brass grommets, polyethylene-foam crown (which makes this an unsinkable hat), the security strap that goes both under your chin and around the back of your head, and a lifetime replacement guarantee add up to a price of $39.

Finally, if you live, as I do, in a place where "summer" is a somewhat dubious term applied to those three months a year of poor sledding, then you may find a felt hat will serve you very well spring, summer, and fall, turning away sun, rain, and the occasional snow squall. Dunn's, L. L. Bean, and Worth and Worth all carry a number of felts well suited for all-season use and running in the $35 to $65 price range, among them the Snowy River, the Rough Rider, and the Indiana Jones. Felt crushers are a much cheaper, lighter alternative but tend to lose their shape fairly quickly.

When I told a man in the hat business that my own summer hat was a green felt with a 3-inch brim and the crown pulled up into a peak, he told me I was crazy, what with all those nice light straws and cotton jobbies out there. Well, I said, the green cuts the glare; and because I'm always around water, I can dunk the hat anytime and cool my head that way. But the real reason I wear it, of course, is that in my youth I came under the spell of a man who could pole a canoe upstream faster than most people could paddle down, knew the woods of western Maine backwards and forwards, went on periodic benders of epic proportion, and wore this same green felt with a 3-inch brim. (The Broadbrim Safari, $39.95 from Dunn's, looks just about like it.)

So if you should decide, contrary to all the good advice I've just given you here, that the summer hat you need is a black felt cowboy hat that will fry your brains under the August sun but that makes you look like Jack Palance in *Shane*, don't worry about it. You've got lots of company. When it comes to hats, mystique will put reason to rout any day.

Where to Buy Them

You'll find hats just about everywhere, from the most discounted discount store on up to the most elegant—and pricey—clothing and specialty shops. Mail order sources are:

CAMPMOR
P.O. Box 997
Paramus, New Jersey 07653-0997
800-526-4784

DUNN'S INC.
Highway 57E
P.O. Box 449
Grand Junction, Tennessee 38039-0449
800-223-8667

L. L. BEAN, INC.
Freeport, Maine 04033
800-221-4221

ORVIS
P.O. Box 12000
Roanoke, Virginia 24022-8001
800-541-3541

RECREATIONAL EQUIPMENT, INC. (REI)
P.O. Box C-88125
Seattle, Washington 98138-2125
800-426-4840

SMITH AND HAWKEN
25 Corte Madera
Mill Valley, California 94941
415-383-2000

TILLEY ENDURABLES
118 Needham Street
Newton Highlands, Massachusetts 02161
800-338-2797

VERMONT COUNTRY STORE
P.O. Box 3000
Manchester Center, Vermont 05255-3000
802-362-2400

WORTH AND WORTH, LTD.
331 Madison Avenue
New York, New York 10017
800-HAT-SHOP

Chore Boots

If there is one chore in the world that is the quintessential chore-boot chore, it is mucking out a cow barn. Chores that are less quintessential but still require boots with similar qualities include hosing down the milk room or slaughterhouse floor, pouring cement, reaming out a drainage ditch with a shovel, extracting the family pickup from a bog hole, or simply going to the mailbox in mud time.

Because you wear chore boots in wet, sticky, sloppy, and sometimes smelly environments, you want the boot to put an impervious layer between you and whatever it is you are wallowing in. You want rubber or plastic boots that will not crack, that are not easily punctured or torn, and that will not give way at the seams. You certainly want the boots to come well up on your leg, preferably just short of the knees, because even if you're not wading that deep, you're probably splashing that high. Sixteen or 17 inches is about right, though for some needs 10 or 12 might be fine.

Chances are you will not want to walk into your kitchen or living room wearing the boots you had on when you cleaned the barn or butchered your pig, so your chore boots should be easy to get on and off. You leave them and whatever may be clinging to them on the back porch or in the mud room, and the next time you go out, you just step into them. Chore boots should not have laces. They complicate putting on and taking off, and their attendant eyes, tongues, and crevices soon become caked with whatever slop you happen to be working in.

We are talking, then, about smooth, straight, almost knee-high, pull-on, kick-off boots that no one would dream of wearing for extended walking but that are the country man or woman's first line of foot defense against muck and manure. A straightforward proposition, it would seem; but there is far more variety available in this apparently simple item than meets the eye. One major reason why that variety rarely meets any of our eyes is that stocking many different kinds of chore boots in many different sizes would take up more space than most stores can give them. So what you're likely to find is only a few models in the most common sizes. But if you know what the possibilities are, you can always special order any boot you want.

Tingley, Servus, and LaCrosse, the three major U.S. manufacturers of protective footwear, offer many options in both materials and styles. The choices in materials are neoprene, PVC, and rubber. Neoprene is comfortable and highly durable. Its resistance to gasoline, kerosene, greases, salts, alcohols, and most oils makes it the material of choice for many industrial uses. Neoprene boots are, however, comparatively expensive (about $45 to $55).

PVC is a material that varies vastly in quality. It may be cheap stuff that stiffens at cool temperatures and tears and cracks at the slightest provocation, or it can be made of high-quality compounds that keep it pliable at all temperatures and make it comfortable and durable. These differences in quality are reflected in suggested retail prices that range from as low as $11 up to about $35. If all you need boots for is to walk from your house to your car in the mud once a month, then a cheap, ill-fitting PVC boot may be just fine. If you want something better, one guide to quality is a good fit, which indicates that the manufacturer gave some careful thought to the last. Better boots will also be in the higher price range ($20 to $35) and will have a soft, rubbery feel.

Because PVC is resistant to acids, salts, and alcohols, it, like neoprene, is often favored for industrial uses. Blending it with other substances can improve its performance for specific tasks and work environments. A PVC/urethane blend is abrasion resistant, hence more durable on concrete floors. Tingley has a PVC/nitrile blend (nitrile is a synthetic rubber) that holds up well to hydrocarbons.

But unless your country life brings your feet into frequent contact with gas, oil, grease, or animal or vegetable fats and oils, the old standby—rubber—will probably be your material of choice. A rubber boot is more comfortable and durable than lower-priced PVC but costs less than neoprene. Here too, however, there is rubber and rubber. If you use your boots hard, both wearing them and leaving them outdoors in the sun where they are subject to greater ozone deterioration, invest $10 or $15 more for an ozone-resistant pair. Tingley's Series 3000 standard rubber knee boots cost about $25. The better grade rubber in the Series 2000 boots raises their price to the $35 to $45 range. LaCrosse's ozone-resistant boots are priced similarly, and though Servus does not talk about ozone resistance, quality and weight of rubber is clearly reflected in its price scale, too. (All prices mentioned here are suggested retail, and depending on where you buy, you will often find significantly lower prices.)

When it comes to styles of rubber boots, the first major distinction is between over-the-sock and over-the-shoe boots. There are relatively few over-the-shoe boots because a work shoe plus a lined, knee-high boot makes a lot of weight to haul around on your feet. However, if you don't have to move around much and want a high, rugged boot you can pull on over your shoes, the LaCrosse 18-inch Denver ($38), 14-inch Utah ($30), the Servus Strap-On ($30.90), or Tingley's Leggin Boot ($25.50) may be what you're looking for. Much lighter is the boot Tingley is justifiably famous for: the 10-inch Work Boot ($18), an extremely tough unlined overboot. Because these boots are so light, compact, and flexible and have no awkward metal clamps, they can be rolled up and stuffed into a pack, the trunk of a car, or a bicycle saddlebag. Tingley also makes a knee-high version of this same boot. LaCrosse has an extensive line of overboots for wear over western boots.

The boots you're more likely to want on the back porch are over-the-sock models, and there are a number of different features available in them apart from the choices of materials. Although all these boots are unlaced pull-ons, different models are cut differently to emphasize different aspects of fit. If ease of entry and exit is your priority, then you'll want a boot that is roomy in the leg and ankle. If, on the other hand, your chores involve a fair amount of walking or you get into the kind of muck that sucks your boots right off you, then you'll want a snugger fit. If you compare Tingley's "knee boots" with its "snugleg" models, the differences are immediately obvious. Where the lines of the knee boots are straight and simple, those of the snuglegs cling closely to the contours of the calf and ankle. LaCrosse describes its boots of this type as "ankle fitting."

Women who want boots built on lasts specifically designed for women's feet will not have a vast range to choose from, but LaCrosse offers two rubber boots for women, and Tingley has a line of women's PVC boots in navy blue, maroon, and gray.

Another feature you can have in any boot, whether of neoprene, PVC, or rubber, is a steel toe. You don't have to lay water mains or work on an oil rig to appreciate the value of that. You may not think your toes are in much danger, but the family cow has to step on your foot only once to make those extra three or five or seven dollars seem an excellent investment indeed. Two other safety options available in some models are a stainless steel midsole (a thin steel plate that protects the entire bottom of the foot from puncture injuries from below) and a metatarsal guard that extends from the steel toe up over the arch of the foot.

Most over-the-sock boots have a steel shank, the primary purpose of which is support. However, it also affords some protection for the arch of your foot if you do occasional digging with your chore boots on. Anyone who expects to do any serious digging with spade, garden fork, or shovel would do well to get a boot with an instep especially reinforced for that purpose. The English Garden Boot ($39 from Smith and Hawken or Plow and Hearth) is an excellent choice for the gardener. Not only does it have a heavy instep pad to prevent arch fatigue, but it also has reinforcing patches at the ankles where the spade rubs. Only 12 inches high, it is cooler than knee-height boots. A few American-made boots that have a reinforced "shovel shank" are Servus's Knee Irrigation Boot and LaCrosse's Economy Short Boot, Short Black Boot, and Brown Short Boot.

Finally, look at the design of the sole itself. There are basically two patterns: fine and heavy. The fine patterns (Tingley's "SafetyLoc," LaCrosse's "Vibram Safety"; Servus's "Neo-grip" is available only in neoprene boots) provide maximum contact for sure, non-skid footing on wet, slippery floors. The heavy soles, variously called "cleated," "tractor tread," "chevron," and so on, provide maximum grip outdoors and are self-cleaning so that they don't fill up with mud and debris. For most country uses, the heavy, lugged soles will be more appropriate.

Where to Buy Them

LaCrosse, Servus, and Tingley products are sold nationwide through farm and garden stores, feed and grain dealers, and many other outlets. Because stores stock so few models, it is important to consult company catalogs if you want to see the full range of boots available. To order a catalog or locate a dealer near you, call or write the companies.

LACROSSE FOOTWEAR, INC.
LaCrosse, Wisconsin 54603
800-323-2668

SERVUS RUBBER COMPANY, INC.
1136 2d Street, Box 36
Rock Island, Illinois 61201

TINGLEY RUBBER CORPORATION
P.O. Box 100
South Plainfield, New Jersey 07080
800-631-5498

English garden boot:

PLOW AND HEARTH
560 Main Street
Madison, Virginia 22727

SMITH AND HAWKEN
25 Corte Madera
Mill Valley, California 94941

COUNTRY FUN

Fishing in the Sky

The expression "Go fly a kite!" has always distressed me. It implies that you're behaving so idiotically that you should get out of sensible people's way and go do something in keeping with your own inane nature; that is, you should go fly a kite, as if kite-flying were the world's biggest waste of time and therefore ideally suited for nitwits like you. Nothing could be further from the truth.

Kite-fliers may be crazy, but they are not stupid. A glance at the list of distinguished kiters is enough to prove that. When Marconi sent his first wireless message across the Atlantic in 1901, the aerial at the receiving station in Newfoundland was carried aloft by a kite. The Wright brothers did a lot of messing around with kites and gliders before they made their first powered flight.

Kites have towed carriages and boats, lofted ads into the sky, and, as at Niagara Falls, made the construction of suspension bridges possible by carrying lines across river gorges. These technological accomplishments are all well and good, but I am personally much more drawn to the mystical and metaphorical aspects of kiting. Anybody who likes to fish as much as I do can't miss the analogy between sinking a line into the water and sending one into the sky, an analogy that is much reinforced by many kiters' adoption of the rod and reel to increase kite maneuverability and make storage and retrieval of line easier. Champion kiter Will Yolen favored this system, and when passers-by saw him sky-fishing in New York's Central Park, they would often ask, "What fish did you catch today?"

"Flying fish," Yolen would snap back.

I can't claim to be much of a kiter, but I've done enough kiting to know the thrills of hooking and playing big windfish on my line in the sky. The natives of Malaysia—people for whom sea and wind were the dominant natural forces—used kites in religious ceremonies to honor the wind god, and it takes no great leap of the imagination to see the kite as man's messenger to heaven, the dwelling place of the gods. Nor is it surprising that kites often take the shape of fish, dragons, and serpents, creatures of both the watery and the mythological deep. In German, the word for kite is *Drachen* (dragon), a usage that goes back to the hollow windsocks that Roman legions carried as standards and that frequently had dragons or serpents painted on them. Even in English, the Latin word *draco* persisted until about 1650, when the collective mind of England must have decided that kites bore a much stronger resemblance to the soaring, hawklike birds of that name than they did to dragons.

But even though *draco* is no longer our favored word for kite, the dragon is still one of the most popular kite designs; and if your local five-and-dime store carries kites, chances are they will be dragons. The dragon is simplicity itself—a hoop shaped something like a croquet wicket, a center spar to attach the bridle to, and a long tail. Dragons are easy to launch and fly; and with tails anywhere from 10 to 100 feet long, they perform spectacular, looping antics in the sky. If you want to hook a kid—or yourself—on kiting, a dragon kite is a surefire bet. You can buy a 25-foot dragon made of Mylar for around $5. A 50-footer runs about $9. Along with the visual effects, you get lovely audible ripplings and rustlings from the Mylar tail, too. If you want more durable dragons, you can spend $25 to $35 for models made with fiberglass frames and nylon taffeta or spinnaker nylon. Spinnaker nylon is a fabric that gets very high marks from kite makers. Not only is it a ripstop nylon, but it is also urethane coated and therefore nonporous. Nylon taffeta is not as strong, and kites made from it tend to be less expensive than similarly sized kites of spinnaker nylon.

A variation on the dragon kite is the octopus, a kite with the same body as the dragon but with a lot of shorter arms instead of one long tail. The overall length is about 6 feet. What the octopus lacks in sky-carving grace, it makes up for in its hula-skirt flutter. The dragon is more elegant; the octopus is cuter. Mylar octopi come in the same price range as dragons, some models going for as little as $3; and they, too, are easy, unfinicky kites to fly.

Another excellent design for beginning kiters is the delta. Like delta-wing airplanes, deltas are flying triangles. They are cut from cloth or polyethylene and reinforced with battens in the leading edges of the wings and with a central spine. A spar extending across the back keeps the wings spread, and the line is attached to a keel. A couple of tattered and disabled polyethylene deltas in my woodshed suggest to me that I might have been better off spending a few more dollars for a cloth model. You can buy small (46- to 54-inch wingspan) ripstop nylon deltas suitable for adults and children for about $12 to $16. Polyethylene ones of that size cost around $5 to $7. The larger the wingspan, the more reliable your delta will be in light winds. Nylon 6-footers go for between $15 and $25, depending on the type of nylon used.

Just about any string, cord, or thread will do for a line, but because the optimal kite line supplies adequate strength with minimal wind resistance and weight, a thin strong line is clearly better than a thick weak one. Monofilament fishing line supplies both qualities, but many kiters shun it for the same reason fishermen curse it: It loves to get hopelessly tangled up in itself. Braided Dacron is the line of choice among hard-core kite buffs. The rule of thumb for strength is that the line should be able to withstand a pull—in pounds—that is three times greater than the area—in square feet—of your kite. For example, a kite with an area of 5 square feet needs a 15-pound test line.

Appealing as I find the idea of flying a kite from a fishing rod, I have to admit there are simpler, cheaper ways to store and reel in your line. The main thing is to have a device that can take in a lot of line at one stroke. Winding a thousand feet of kite line onto a ¼-inch dowel can take all the fun out of kiting. My own simple expedient is a board about a foot long and 6 to 8 inches wide. I round off the edges to prevent abrasion of the line and wind the line on the board lengthwise, which means that for each complete turn I retrieve 2 feet of line. Valerie Govig, editor of *Kite Lines* magazine, favors the Halo hoop, a simple plastic hoop on which you wind your line. Halo hoops come in 7-, 8-, and 9-inch diameters (listed in *Into the Wind*'s catalog at $3.75, $4.90, and $7.50).

In kiting, the sky is your only limit, and whether you build your own kites out of shopping bags and paper plates, buy high-tech kites, or do both, you'll know what sky-fisherman Will Yolen meant when he said the sensation of flying a kite is like holding the wind in your hands.

Reading about Kites

Kite Lines, a quarterly journal published by the Aeolus Press, Inc., with editorial offices at 7106 Campfield Road, Baltimore, Maryland 21207-4699, is a major nerve center of the international kiting community. If there is anything you want to know about kites and kiting, you can find it either in or through *Kite Lines*. The magazine has a directory of kite stores in the United States and abroad, and it also operates a mail-order bookstore that stocks kiting literature from all over the world.

If there is one book every kiter needs, it is *The Penguin Book of Kites* by David Pelham (New York: Penguin Books, 1976, $9.95). This "kiteflier's bible" covers kite history, construction, and flying and provides plans for building many kites.

An excellent short book is Wyatt Brummitt's *Kites* (New York: Golden Press, 1971). Originally published as a Golden Guide, this book was out of print for many years, but *Kite Lines* issued a new, updated edition of it in March 1987.

Mail-order Sources for Kites and Kite Supplies

CATCH THE WIND
266 S.E. Highway 101
Lincoln City, Oregon 97367

FISH CREEK KITE COMPANY
3853 Highway 42
Fish Creek, Wisconsin 54212

GO FLY A KITE
Box AA
East Haddam, Connecticut 06423

HEAVENLY BODY KITES
409 Greene Street
Key West, Florida 33040

HI FLI KITES
12101-C East Iliff
Aurora, Colorado 80014

HIGH FLY KITE COMPANY
33 Evergreen Lane
Haddonfield, New Jersey 08033

INTO THE WIND
2047 Broadway
Boulder, Colorado 80302

KITES AWEIGH
6 Fleet Street
Annapolis, Maryland 21401

THE KITE SITE
3101 M Street NW
Washington, D.C. 20007

THE UNIQUE PLACE
525 S. Washington at 6th
Royal Oak, Michigan 48067

Cross-Country Skis

"Nordic" seems to be winning out over "cross-country" as the adjective to describe all those skis you can use without benefit of a chair lift, gondola, or condominium. I applaud that trend in usage because, of the roughly 250 models of Nordic skis on the market today, probably only a quarter to a third of them are cross-country skis in the traditional sense. A cross-country ski is, by my definition, just that: a ski for travelling through field and forest, up hill and down dale, a ski for going where few other people go and where you may have to break your own trail through deep powder, use your skis as impromptu bridges across small brooks, whack your way through brush, and, depending on your local climate and the time of year, ski on everything from armor-plated crust to refrozen corn to slush. The racer's javelin-shaped skating skis are not designed for those conditions, nor are many of the slender performance skis that are great fun to use for an aerobic workout on the groomed trails of a touring center. Nor will the average cross-country skier need the opposite extreme of the very widest mountaineering skis.

Width and shape are the main things that distinguish a cross-country ski from its Nordic cousins; but before you start thinking about dimensions, you first have to decide between a waxable or a no-wax ski. In my mind, there is no choice. Waxable skis are vastly superior. But roughly 75 percent of the Nordic skis sold in this country are waxless. Why? Beginning skiers are drawn to waxless skis because they can just put them on under any snow and weather conditions and go skiing. They picture themselves gliding off into a glorious winter day while the waxers are still messing around with their funny little cakes of wax.

There is some small truth to that picture, but the greater truth is that just about anyone I've ever skied with who was using waxless skis has soon asked me, "Why is it that you're gliding farther than I am, going faster, working less, and having more fun?" Even beginners quickly realize that the convenience of waxless skis does not compensate for their poorer performance. Then, too, waxing is nowhere near the big deal it is made out to be. In the sustained cold weather of mid-winter, you may not have to touch your wax job from one week to the next, and if the weather does get shifty on you, experienced skiers are always glad to share waxing strategies that work for your local snow conditions.

To sum up: If you won't use your skis more than four or five times a year, you'll probably be quite content with waxless skis. If, on the other hand, you ski more like two to five times a week, you'll soon be trading in for waxable skis.

When I bought my first pair of cross-country skis, the choices of materials were wood, wood, and wood. Now the only all-wood skis I know of are the Asnes Fjellski and Tur/Langrenn. All other skis are made of synthetics. But wood remains the superior material. Wooden skis have a life, a liveliness, a responsiveness that no synthetics do. If other experienced skiers hadn't told me they feel the same way, I would suspect myself of retrograde nature worship and an overwrought reverence for wood. But I am far from alone in preferring my old woodies for skiing on the silky powder of January and February.

In New England, though, those perfect snow conditions can disappear overnight. A thaw followed by a freeze-up can change powder to crusty, scratchy stuff that acts like coarse sandpaper on wooden skis. Nor do I like exposing my wooden skis to the slush, grit, and mud of March and April, but it is a crime not to be out skiing on those long, warm spring days. The synthetic-fiber skis that now dominate the market offer a way out of that dilemma. They can take great punishment and show little damage from it, and they are easy to maintain. The moral is simple. If you can buy only one pair of skis, buy synthetics that you can use under any and all conditions. If you have some spare change, treat yourself to a pair of woodies for the cold-weather powder.

I've been using the term "synthetics" rather recklessly here to take in an immense variety of construction possibilities: wood cores, foam cores, aluminum honeycomb cores, fiberglass laminations, ABS top skins, sintered or extruded bases of polyethylene or polyurethane, to mention only a few. Complex as the whole business appears, the buyer who avoids the cheap $100 package and gets a middle to top-line ski needn't fret about any of it too much. I happen to prefer a wood core for the same reasons I like an all-wood ski: liveliness and snappiness. I also want metal edges to give me control on ice and hard pack and to hold up against the abrasion that literally grinds the edges off an unprotected ski. Sintered bases have large pores and hold wax better than extruded bases, but again just about any high quality ski will hold wax decently.

For the cross-country-ski buyer, size, shape, weight, and action are more crucial than understanding details of construction. A cross-country ski should be rugged and stable, turn easily, and provide enough flotation to keep you from sinking to your hips in soft snow. Skis that fill this bill have traditionally been called "touring" and "light touring" skis. Other terms you may find applied to skis of this type are "recreational," "off-track," and "telemark/mountaineering." But regardless of name, what you'll be looking at will be skis ranging from about 44- to 50-millimeters wide at the waist (the narrowest part of the ski) in the light touring class and from about 50- to 57-mm in touring. If you favor the unbroken snows of the backcountry, you'll want a relatively wide touring ski with ample sidecut. Sidecut is what determines ease in turning. It is the inward curve that runs from the shovel of the ski (the widest part of the tip), tapers down to the narrowest point at the waist, and widens out again toward the tail. There are no iron-clad limits on sidecut, but in a touring ski it will typically run 7 to 12 mm. My own two pairs of touring skis measure (at shovel, waist, and tail) 61/51/57 and 68/56/64. If you spend more time on prepared trails than in the woods, you may be happier with a slimmer, light touring ski with a little less sidecut, say, 52/48/50.

Once you've settled on a touring or light touring ski and decided to go waxable or waxless, you next have to select a specific ski that fits you. What you want is a ski with the proper *camber stiffness* for you. Camber is the upward curve in the middle of the ski, and I run it together with stiffness because it is best to think of camber stiffness as a single concept and the measure of it as the downward force required to flatten out the camber of the ski. If the camber stiffness of your skis is right, the force of your kick should drive the center of the ski (the "wax pocket" on a waxable ski or the grippers on a waxless one) firmly enough down into the snow to give you a solid push-off. Conversely, when you are gliding either on one foot or two, the camber should be stiff enough to unweight the center of the ski slightly, reducing friction and so enhancing glide. If you are going to err at all, it's better to choose a ski that is a little too soft rather than one a little too stiff. The penalty for a soft ski is reduction in speed, not a crucial factor in bushwhacking. The penalty for too much camber stiffness is the inability to climb hills and maybe even some difficulty on the flat.

The traditional method of fitting skis is to stand with your arm up in the air and pick a ski that reaches your wrist. Ski manufacturers try to match ski length and camber stiffness to the average weight range of people of given heights, and this selection method may give you a ski that is just right for you. But it is obviously far from precise. If, for instance, you are skinny and light for your height, you may well need a ski 5 centimeters shorter (and therefore softer) than the arm-up-in-the-air test would suggest.

A test for camber stiffness you can try in a store goes like this:

On a clean, hard, perfectly flat floor, place a strip of paper about 4 inches wide under the middle of one ski of a pair. Now stand on the skis with your feet where the bindings would go and with your weight evenly divided between the two skis. If there is some resistance when you pull the paper out, the camber stiffness is about right. With all your weight on the one ski, you should not be able to move the paper at all.

The help of a truly knowledgeable salesperson is invaluable in selecting skis, but, unfortunately, good sales advice on Nordic skis is not always easy to come by. Shops specializing in downhill ski gear may have some Nordic skis as a sideline and not know or care much about them. Your chances of finding savvy sales people are much better at a specialty Nordic ski shop or one associated with a cross-country touring center. Also, if dealers in your area have demo days, go out and ski on everything they've got. There's no better test than trying before you buy.

Finding the Right Skis

The most thorough and current introduction to the construction, characteristics, and selection of modern Nordic skis is in Michael Brady's *Cross-Country Ski Gear* (2d edition, 1987), available directly from The Mountaineers Books, 306 Second Avenue West, Seattle, Washington 98119, 800-553-4453, for $9.95.

For an up-to-date survey of skis, boots, and poles, see *Cross-Country Skier* magazine's annual buyer's guide, published each November.

The "good, better, best" scheme applies in Nordic skis, and you'll often find skis of identical dimensions sold in three different grades. The Trak Sportive, Nova, and Runner, for example, are all 55/50/52 waxless skis with suggested retail prices of $140, $180, and $200. You'll find prices in those ranges right across the market in both waxable and waxless skis, but better grade and wider back-country and mountaineering skis with metal edges can go well above the $200 mark. You can beat those prices by shopping at the Great-End-of-Winter Washington's Birthday Sales or by watching for second-hand sales.

The Incomplete Angler

A popular bumper sticker in my part of the country says "A bad day of fishing is still better than a good day at work." My sentiments precisely, so much so that I can hardly imagine how bad a day of fishing would have to get for me to call it "bad." But a hard-core maniac introducing a beginner to the sport soon learns that it takes very little adversity to make a bad day of fishing for the unaddicted. So if you want to raise your children to be fisherfolk or to convert a mate or dear friend, see to it that they don't have bad days. Keep them comfortable; equip them with tackle that they can master easily; and make sure they catch lots of fish.

The freshwater fish most likely to help you follow that last rule are the plentiful and voracious creatures often lumped together under the heading of "panfish": bluegills, crappies, yellow perch, white perch. They will eat just about anything you throw at them at just about any time you care to throw it. As for tackle, there is still much to be said for a long bamboo pole with a length of monofilament line tied to the tip, a bobber, a number 10 or 12 hook, and a can of worms. There is no reel and long line to get tangled up in, yet the length of the pole plus about an equal length of line gives you ample reach for panfish. For an outlay of a few dollars, you have a simple, serviceable outfit. Telescoping fiberglass versions of the old bamboo pole cost around $15 in the 10- to 14-foot sizes; some are equipped with a rudimentary reel.

But pleasant as still fishing with a pole may be, it is limiting; and just about any beginner will soon want to try casting with a rod and reel. Freshwater fishing tackle is categorized by the kind of casting you can do with it: fly casting, spinning, spin casting, and bait casting. In spinning or bait casting, the line is light, and the lure is relatively heavy. The rod is used like a catapult to toss that heavy lure out where you want it to go, the lure pulling the lightweight line behind it. In fly fishing, it's the line that supplies the weight; the action and leverage of the long rod are used to throw the *line*, not the lure, which is practically weightless. The reel's major function is just to hold the line.

In spinning, the reel is mounted underneath the rod with an exposed or open-faced spool parallel to the rod. When you cast, the spool remains stationary as the line is pulled off the end of it. The bait-casting reel is mounted on top of the rod with its spool at right angles to the rod. When you cast, the spool turns as the line is pulled off it. You control the speed at which it turns by pressing on the spool with your thumb. Many modern bait-casting reels have mechanical thumb bars and magnetic braking systems that help prevent the spool from spinning faster than the line goes out.

Spin casting, as its name suggests, is a cross between spinning and bait casting. It uses a reel that is mounted on top of the rod, as in bait casting, but that has a spool parallel to the rod, as in spinning. Spin-casting reels, however, are closed-face, that is, they have a cone-shaped cover over the spool, and the line runs out through a hole at the tip of the cone.

Despite all the high-tech gadgetry and mumbo jumbo associated with fly casting and, to a lesser extent, bait casting, they are not arts beyond the reach of normal mortals. But because instant gratification is what you want for beginners, especially for children, start them out with spinning or spin-casting tackle. Spinning makes using a vast variety of lures so easy that it has virtually replaced bait casting for most weekend anglers. Spin casting is, if anything, even easier than spinning, so for a child of roughly kindergarten age, spin-casting tackle is probably a good choice for a first outfit. A thumb trigger on the reel releases the line for casting, and the closed face helps prevent snarls and snags. No great dexterity is needed to get quite decent results. Zebco, the major manufacturer of spin-casting reels, has gone so far in its pursuit of the young set as to produce Snoopy and Mickey Mouse outfits in which a spin-cast reel is molded right into the handle of a rod. Price, including 8-pound-test monofilament line: about $10.

For a child of eight or nine (or a precocious younger one), start out with spinning tackle. It is only slightly more difficult to master than spin-casting tackle but more satisfying to use. Both spinning and spin-casting packages complete with rod, reel, and line are a common sight in most discount stores and in many large drugstores. You won't get classy, last-a-lifetime tackle in such stores, but until someone is really hooked on fishing, it's foolish to spend a lot of money. For $25 or $35, sometimes for a little as $15 or $20, you can get a passable, entry-level package; but discount stores tend to have tackle too heavy for most beginners' needs.

The labels on most spinning and spin-casting rods classify their action as ultra light, light, medium, or heavy. For panfishing, medium is too heavy for my tastes. However, medium rods that take 6-, 8-, and 10-pound test lines are often recommended for young children who may tend to yank hard, break a lighter test line, and get discouraged by losing fish and lures. But the lighter the line, the easier it is to cast light panfishing lures and the more fun it is to play small fish. Most rods have their length and action, the weights of the lines, and the weights of the lures they are designed to handle printed on them just above the grip. For example, a spinning rod that says "6 foot, medium/light, 4- to 10-pound test, ⅛-⅝ oz." would be a good all-around beginner's rod for panfish and on up to good-sized bass and pickerel. For someone with some experience, a light or ultralight outfit that takes 2- to 6-pound test line would be even more fun.

A child who starts out catching a lot of panfish on worms and light spinning lures but sees an adult catching these same fish on a fly rod will naturally want to learn fly fishing, too. The best way for either child or adult to learn is, of course, to go out and fish with someone who knows how. An old hand can select suitable tackle, ease the beginner into good casting habits, and see to it that he or she keeps catching some fish.

If such a mentor is not available, an introductory fly-fishing school can teach sound casting technique from the start, sparing beginners months and years of frustration and keeping them from developing bad habits they'll have to unlearn later. For the autodidact, there are some superb videos that supplement basic books and convey casting technique better than the written word can.

Specialty tackle retailers often offer basic fly-fishing outfits at very reasonable prices. L. L. Bean sells the outfit it uses in its introductory fly-fishing school for $89. The package includes a 7½-, 8-, or 8½-foot rod, a reel, the proper weight line for the rod, line backing, leader, and Dave Whitlock's *Fly-Fishing Handbook*, a concise but comprehensive guide to fly fishing.

Resources

Mail-order Sources

CABELA'S
812 13th Avenue
Sidney, Nebraska 69160

Spinning, spin-casting, bait-casting, and fly-casting tackle.

THE HOOK AND HACKLE COMPANY
P.O. Box 1003
Plattsburgh, New York 12901

Fly-fishing tackle only.

L. L. BEAN, INC.
Freeport, Maine 04033

Extensive fly-fishing tackle, some spinning, bait-casting, and spin-casting tackle.

THE ORVIS COMPANY
Manchester, Vermont 05254

Primarily fly-fishing tackle, some spinning tackle.

Schools

L. L. BEAN FLY-FISHING SCHOOLS
L. L. Bean, Inc.
Freeport, Maine 04033

Introductory, Intermediate, and Advanced Schools.
Call 800-341-4341, ext. 3100, for detailed information.

ORVIS FLY-FISHING SCHOOL
Manchester, Vermont 05254

All levels.
Call 800-548-9548 for details.

Books and Videos

L. L. Bean Fly-Fishing Handbook by Dave Whitlock, $8.95. 70-minute companion video *L. L. Bean Introduction to Fly Fishing,* featuring Dave Whitlock, $29.95.

L. L. Bean Fly Fishing for Bass Handbook by Dave Whitlock, $8.95. 42-minute companion video *Flyfishing for Bass,* with Dave Whitlock, $24.95.

3M Company/Scientific Anglers has an extensive video series on fishing. Levels range from beginner to expert with titles like *Fly Fishing Made Easy* ($19.95) and *Basic Fly Casting* ($29.95) to *Advanced Fly Casting* ($49.95). For a complete listing or to order, write:

3M LEISURE TIMES PRODUCTS
3M Center
224-2S-27
St. Paul, Minnesota 55144

Wooden Toys

If you'd like to buy some wooden toys for your favorite children this Christmas, you're likely to come up dry at your local Toys R' Us emporium. You will find there, however, a lot of Robot Action Figures, Rambo Helicopter Cockpits, Survivor Ultimate Weapon Systems, and Realistic Play Foods (plastic Dunkin' Donuts, for example, or a plastic Burger King Whopper complete with plastic roll, lettuce, and tomato). But don't despair. Wooden toys still do exist. Toymakers are still making them, and both adults and children still delight in them for the reasons they always have.

Much of the pleasure a wooden toy provides comes from the material itself. Wood grain is intrinsically beautiful, and in consort with the shape the toymaker gives the toy, it makes for an object that never loses its visual appeal. Wooden toys are also durable and, short of total destruction, endlessly repairable. A broken wheel on a truck or a missing smokestack on a train can always be replaced. And so wooden toys often are passed on from generation to generation, acquiring the value of heirlooms. A wooden toy can be broken or destroyed; but, unlike a plastic toy, it can never become junk. It once grew from the earth, and, by way of fire or decay, it can be returned to it.

The relative simplicity of design and execution the material imposes means that children can see and readily comprehend the functioning of simple machines incorporated into toys: wheels, cranks, eccentrics, inclined planes, levers; and they can see how the energy of the wind on a sail or weathervane or whirligig or of water on a waterwheel is translated mechanically into work. Spinning a wooden top, pushing a wooden truck, or pulling a wooden toy train a child acquires physical skills, develops an appreciation for natural materials, and learns basic lessons about human effort and results achieved. Wooden toys help cultivate a sense of proportion, a respect for natural materials and elemental forces, and an awareness of simple work processes, none of which, it seems to me, can be developed with the aid of a Rambo Helicopter Cockpit.

Finally, wooden toys create a special personal bond between the giver and the child. That is particularly so if a parent, other relative, or older friend makes the toy. All wooden toys were originally made at home and modeled on familiar creatures and farm implements: wagons, sleighs, child-sized furniture, windmills, whittled figurines of domestic and wild animals. They were both tokens of affection and the child's first introduction into the family's way of life and work. This special human significance is still inherent in a homemade wooden toy, and it accounts for the continuing interest people have in toymaking today and for the flood of books available on the subject. That significance is not as great in a toy you buy, but even there the material and the craft tradition create palpable values that simply cannot be found in a plastic toy.

If you want to buy rather than make toys, you may have to step off the beaten path. As I've suggested, the mass-market toy outlets are unlikely sources; and even small stores specializing in toys—ones where the owners give some real thought to what is in their inventory—may choose to give only limited shelf space to wooden toys. However, in such stores you are likely to find some modestly priced old favorites, many of them under the Playskool label. A set of 30 lettered wooden blocks, for example, sells for about $8; and the old "Cobbler's Bench"—the child uses a small wooden hammer to drive slotted wooden pegs back and forth through holes in the bench—costs about $7. I still can't pass one of those by without taking a few whacks at a peg or two.

Basic Lincoln Log sets, also by Playskool, range from about $12 for a 72-piece set to about $30 for a 212-piece one. And a Beginner's Set of Tinker Toys, with plans for thirteen toys a child can build with the parts, costs only about $8. These simple toys that evoke a child's inventiveness have not lost their appeal in the jet age. Just a few nights ago I saw a group of kids aged 4 to 16 happily spend a couple of hours with a big set of Lincoln Logs.

These are mass-produced toys, and though they are primarily wooden (there are some plastic parts), they are not what you would call finely crafted. "Mass produced" and "crafted" would seem to be mutually exclusive, and by and large they are. However, there are some wooden toys, produced in large quantities and marketed nationally, whose designs and workmanship certainly earn them a place very close to the craft end of the scale; and they are priced accordingly. Examples are the Brio Wooden Railway sets. The simplest one contains eight sections of interlocking wooden track, a tiny locomotive, and two cars behind it. Price, $26.50. A larger set with some station buildings, overpasses, and underpasses goes for $135. The possibilities for additions are endless: bridges, switches, villages, farms, trees, tank trucks, bulldozers, as many sections of new track as your treasury can afford. The fun is combining the tracks in as many ornate configurations as the child can devise.

A toy that encourages that same impulse in three dimensions is Blocks and Marbles. The different shaped blocks of walnut, maple, and ash in this toy have grooves, tunnels, and channels cut in them, and they can be built up into ornate structures with all kinds of interconnected tunnels through which the marbles can be rolled. High-powered executive types have been known to take this one to work with them, leave instructions that they are not to be disturbed, and then, in the privacy of their offices, quietly proceed to lose their marbles for an hour or two. The starter set with fourteen blocks and seven marbles retails for $13.95. The school set with 192 wooden pieces is the largest and costs $255. In between, there are a number of other sets of varying sizes and prices. Blocks and Marbles is sold nationwide at upscale toy and gift shops, and some sets are available through mail-order sources, such as Recreational Equipment, Inc. (P.O. Box 88125, Seattle, Washington 98138-2125, 800-426-4840), which has a twenty-one-block set for $22.

Interesting wooden toys are as likely to turn up in gift shops or in shops specializing in wood products as they are in toy stores, especially if you live in an area where wood is a major natural resource and woodworking skills have a long tradition behind them. In such shops you will often find not only nationally marketed toys but also toys made by small companies or local crafts people who may not market outside their own state or region. The Once a Tree stores in Camden and Portland, Maine, West Lebanon, New Hampshire, and Burlington, Vermont, offer some beautiful wooden-pig piggybanks, music boxes, airplanes, and novelties from Maine, Vermont, and Missouri producers who do not appear in national directories of toymakers.

There is no lack of fine wooden toys to buy if you know where to find them, but, for the reasons already suggested, I am a great fan of the homemade toy. Fortunately, both knowledge and supplies are readily available to the amateur toymaker. An invaluable resource is Cherry Tree Toys, Inc., P.O. Box 369, Belmont, Ohio 43718, 614-484-4363, which offers plans for a vast number of toys including whirligigs; riding toys; floor and sandbox toys like steam-shovels, cars, trucks, trains, planes, and bulldozers; animal pull toys (rabbits, frogs, and grasshoppers that hop; dogs that run; hippos that open their mouths); doll furniture and doll houses. For many of these toys, Cherry Tree also has kits that require different amounts of labor and expertise from the purchaser. Precut kits supply all the parts for a particular toy. You just sand, glue, and finish. Uncut kits supply the turned pieces and uncut stock for the toy. Parts-required kits supply only turned parts or ones that are especially hard to make. If you have no woodworking experience, you can start with a precut kit, then start graduating back to uncut kits, parts-required kits, plans only, and, eventually, to your own toys designed and built from scratch.

Cherry Tree also has an extensive line of hard-to-make parts, like wheels, smokestacks, and cams, as well as hardware for toys, toymakers' tools, and special nontoxic paints and oil finishes. Last but far from least is a good selection of books on woodworking skills and on building many different types of toys.

Wooden Toy Safety

Because young children are prone to putting things in their mouths, they are most susceptible to the hazards wooden toys—or any other toys—may present: toxic ingredients (lead, cadmium, or selenium, for example) in paints, lacquers, and oils, and small parts that the child can swallow and choke on. Such parts may be intentionally detachable, such as miniature barrels on a toy truck, or they may be parts like small wheels or headlights that can be easily broken or bitten off the toy. Long ropes on pull toys make entanglement and strangulation possible. Sharp edges, sharp corners, splinters, or sharp hardware are also obvious hazards.

The U.S. Consumer Product Safety Commission issues mandatory standards for the nontoxicity and sturdiness of toys; and the Toy Manufacturers of America (TMA), the toy industry trade association, has developed its own voluntary safety standards program. The TMA publishes two free pamphlets on toy safety, the selection of appropriate toys for different age levels, and the age grading and age labeling used in the toy industry. For *The ABC's of Toys and Play* and *Learning about Labels,* send a postcard to Toy Booklets, P.O. Box 866, Madison Square Station, New York, New York 10159.

Ultimately, however, choosing safe toys is a parental responsibility, and no commission or industry program can relieve parents of it. And that, of course, is an added benefit of making your own toys. If you put Behlen's Salad Bowl Finish on a toy yourself—or no finish at all—then you know you have a nontoxic surface.

Toymaking Books

The Great All-American Wooden Toy Book by Norm Marshall (Emmaus, Pennsylvania: Rodale Press, 1986), $10.95, stands out for the detail and specificity of its instructions and the elegance of its designs. Its Model-T truck, bulldozer, and road grader are the handsomest I've ever seen.

Whirligigs: Design and Construction by Anders S. Lunde, 2d ed. (Radnor, Pennsylvania: Chilton Book Co., 1986), $10.95, offers a detailed introduction to different types of wind toys (winged, arm-waving, mechanical) as well as designs for human figures (Colonial Dame, Soldier).

How to Make Animated Toys by David Wakefield (New York: Sterling Publishing, 1986), $12.95, explains the simple machines, like cams and eccentrics, that can be used to impart special motions to animated toys and includes designs such as a Hopping Rabbit and a Bouncing Bus.

Camping Saws

A friend of mine who recently took an Allagash River canoe trip reported to me that the guide who led the expedition had devised a novel way of keeping his party in firewood for the ten-day trip. That is no mean trick because, as you will know if you are familiar with the wild and untamed Allagash, the hordes who pass there each year have long since scoured at least some of the campsites clean of every last combustible stick.

With the canoes launched and loaded at the put-in, guide and guests scouted out three good-sized, standing dead cedar. The guide pulled his chain saw out of his truck, dismembered the trees, split them up into bite-sized pieces, and stuffed them into every last nook and cranny in the canoes. "And you know," my friend said, "he figured things just right. He burned the last stick of that wood to cook the last flapjack of the trip."

So in the waning years of the twentieth century if you ask "What saw will the knowledgeable woodsman or woodswoman carry into the bush?" the answer you'll get may well be "A Homelite 360," though it is not the answer you'll get from me. The chain saw is not, of course, the only device that is displacing the hand-held, hand-powered camp saw. The word "saw" simply does not appear in the indexes of books on backpacking, and the entries under "fires" will usually be "difficulty of starting," "inconvenience of," "environmental damage caused by," "offensiveness of to the ecologically high-minded," and so on. The argument is that campfires are simply passé and you should carry a stove. There's some justification for that argument. In dry, open, heavily traveled country where wood is scarce, the danger of forest fire high, and the black blotch of a campfire an eyesore, the little backpacking stove makes real sense.

But let's assume that you are miles from the nearest chain saw and that you just plain like campfires. You're on a river or lake in the boreal north where there is standing deadwood galore, the woods are sodden from a week's rain, and you can build your fire on a gravel beach. If you are or ever will be such a person in such a place, you'll want a compact, efficient saw in your kit.

A good trail saw should be collapsible, folding into a small package that weighs next to nothing and can slip neatly into a pack or wanigan. When the saw is folded, the teeth of the blade should be sheathed in an absolutely foolproof way so that they cannot escape and saw up the contents of your pack. It's also nice if the saw, unfolded, is capable of producing lots of firewood quickly with a minimum of strain on you. That last requirement disqualifies the breed of folding saw—often billed as a pruning and camping saw—that has a plastic handle and a curved, Teflon-coated blade, looks something like a big switchblade knife, and sells for about $11. Quite apart from the poor design, which forces you to hold this tool as if it were a knife, not a saw, the 7-inch blade is too short to do any serious sawing.

The metal bow saws that are a standard item in hardware stores don't fit the bill either. The usual blade lengths are 21, 24, 30, and 36 inches. The larger models are too big and awkward for carrying in anything but a truck or car; the blade has to be protected with some kind of makeshift sheath, such as a length of old garden hose split on one side and then tied onto the blade; and the handle design is inefficient. These saws are meant to be used with two hands, but the bow is too shallow and keeps the hands too close together for good control. The 21- and 24-inch models are one-handed tools and much more manageable, but even a small bow saw is still a nuisance to pack. Also, the smaller models often have triangular or nearly triangular frames, which, depending on the diameter of the wood you're cutting, reduces the length of your stroke as you saw through the stick.

For only a few dollars more you can buy a Sven-Saw with a 21-inch blade. This all-metal saw folds into a flat package 1½ by 23 inches and weighs 13 ounces. The tooth pattern is a mini version of the pattern used in the huge 6-foot, two-man crosscut saws—four cutting teeth to a raker—and the Sven-Saw will zip quickly and effortlessly through the 2½- to 3-inch wood ideal for firewood billets.

The Sven-Saw's one disadvantage is its triangular frame, which makes finishing off wood four inches in diameter or larger difficult. Also, because the angle between the handle and the blade is too acute (65 degrees), energy that should be expended only in moving the saw back and forth is misdirected down onto the blade.

The Sven-Saw comes in a model with a 15-inch blade, too. Given the triangular frame, that length blade makes for a very short stroke in thick wood; and the two ounces in weight and the few inches in length that you save when the saw is folded are not worth the loss in cutting efficiency. Nor is the 15-inch model cheaper than its big brother. Both saws retail for about $14.

If you want a saw that will let you cut larger diameter wood and give you the aesthetic pleasures of a hardwood handle as well, you'll want a folding bucksaw. Like the old pulpwood cutter's bucksaw, the wooden parts of these saws are arranged in an H pattern. The blade extends across the two bottom legs of the H, and a tension bar with wing nuts on it goes across the top. By tightening the wing nuts, you put tension on the blade and clamp the crosspiece of the H firmly in place. When you fold the saw, the blade fits into slits in the handles for safe packing. With the crosspiece and tension bar tied into place, the saw forms a compact unit about 2 inches wide. Folding bucksaws are slightly bulkier and heavier than the Sven-Saw, but the angle of 85 degrees between the handles and the blade makes them much easier and more efficient to use.

The best buy you'll find in folding bucksaws is the Schmidt Packsaw. Peter Schmidt was inspired to develop this saw about thirty years ago when a camping bucksaw he was using literally fell apart in his hands. "Hell," he thought, "I can build a better saw than that." So he did, and he still does. Available in two sizes, Schmidt Packsaws have hand-crafted, red oak handles. The tension bar is an aluminum alloy. For $15.40 (postpaid east of the Mississippi) you can buy a 17-ounce saw with a 24-inch, raker-tooth blade; for $18.45, one with a 30-inch, straight-toothed blade. The space between the blade and the crosspiece on the 24-inch saw is 6¾ inches, which lets you cut some hefty wood. This is a wonderfully simple, sturdy, and effective tool.

Canoe campers in the Midwest have recognized the virtues of this design, too. Paul Swanstrom of Hastings, Minnesota, makes the Fast Bucksaw in both hard maple ($27.25 plus shipping) and cherry ($29.75). Both saws weigh about 17 ounces and have 21-inch, straight-toothed blades and hand-rubbed oil finishes. The Fast Bucksaw is handsomely crafted. All the edges are rounded; the crossbar has pegs in it that help hold the saw firmly together when folded; the tension bar has L-shaped clips on it that protect the wood when the saw is in use and lock the tension bar to the crossbar when the saw is folded. All that attention to detail is of course reflected in the higher price of this saw. The fine workmanship had one serious drawback on the Fast Bucksaw I used, however. The slit into which the blade folds was too narrow. When the saw got wet (as a saw on a rainy canoe trip is bound to), the wood swelled, clamping the blade inside.

Indiana Camp Supply Inc. sells a similar saw, also with a 21-inch blade, for $31.25 plus shipping. This saw is heavier (25 ounces) and bulkier and lacks the fine touches of the Fast Bucksaw.

It's a good idea to make a canvas sheath for any folding saw if you plan to put it in a pack with soft duffle. The blade is hidden away and will not damage either a pack or its contents, but the Sven-Saw has a few sharp corners, and the hardware of the wooden saws can abrade cloth, too. If you'll toss your saw into a wanigan or packbasket along with your cooking pots, then the sheath is superfluous.

Saw Sources

Sven-Saws are available in most stores that specialize in camping gear, also from many mail-order sources. A few are:

CAMPMOR
P.O. Box 997-8
Paramus, New Jersey 07653-0997

L. L. BEAN, INC.
Freeport, Maine 04033

RECREATIONAL EQUIPMENT, INC. (REI)
P.O. Box 88125
Seattle, Washington 98138-2125

Folding bucksaws are available from the following sources:

Schmidt Packsaw
CURTIS-STEBBINS CAMP AND TRAIL EQUIPMENT
RR 1, Box 272
Denmark, Maine 04022

Fast Bucksaw
THE FAST BUCKSAW
110 East 5th Street
Hastings, Minnesota 55033

Collapsible Buck Saw
INDIANA CAMP SUPPLY INC.
P.O. Box 211
Hobart, Indiana 46342

Webs for Walking

The origins of skis and snowshoes are, as the TV documentary might put it, lost in the mists of time. About all the archaeologists can tell us with any degree of certainty is that the people who migrated to North America via the land bridge across the Bering Strait became snowshoers while the folks who stayed home in Eurasia became skiers. No skis slithered across American snows until sometime in the 1800s when a Swedish woodsman, weary of slogging around on the logging trails of Maine or Michigan on outsized tennis rackets, said, "God daam snöshös," tossed his webbed feet into the fire, and set about whittling himself a pair of skis just like the ones he'd had at home.

Skis give you speed at a modest investment in energy. Snowshoes give you control, stability, and maneuverability. If you want to get from one Swedish farmhouse to the next with maximum efficiency, you'll develop the ski. If, however, you are an Iroquois or a Cree who has to live in the winter bush—cut firewood, set traps, fetch water, haul a toboggan—you'll choose snowshoes any day.

The same factors that led native Americans to develop so many different sizes and designs of snowshoes are the same ones a modern recreational snowshoer has to consider in choosing snowshoes today. What is your primary use? How much do you weigh? What kind or kinds of snow will you encounter?

At one end of the design spectrum is the long, skinny Alaskan, or pickerel, snowshoe, which, with its sharply upturned toe, looks something like a short, web-filled ski. At the other end are the flat, nearly round designs, usually called the Montagnais or beavertail. Right in the middle is the Maine (or Michigan) style, and this is the design most people will probably picture when they hear the word "snowshoe." The Maine snowshoe has the shape of an elongated tear drop. It is broad forward, slimmer to the rear, and has a tail and a slightly upturned toe. The variations can be endless: slightly wider, slightly longer, a slightly flatter toe, and so on. The "bearpaw" is a short, broad, tailless shoe that falls between the Maine and the beavertail. The Green Mountain bearpaw, like the basic bearpaw, also lacks a tail, but it tends more toward the Alaskan design in being long and untapered.

The long, skinny snowshoe—like its visual relative, the ski—is a good traveling shoe. Because it is narrow, the feet remain comfortably close together, and the long tail keeps the toe up and the shoe tracking. If you are chopping wood, however, that length makes it easier to cut your own (snowshoe) toes off; it can also make descents on steep hills faster than you expect and ascents slipperier. The bearpaws and beavertails clearly have the edge for working and puttering around a camp. The Maine or Michigan shoe is probably so popular because it has the versatility of a design midway between the extremes.

One of the great snowshoe myths is that bearpaws give you greater maneuverability over longer shoes with tails if you have to travel in thick brush. I've never found this to be true. Width will hang you up as much as length, and if a 10-by-56-inch Alaskan shoe or a 13-by-45-inch Maine can't go through a thicket, chances are a 14-by-30-inch bearpaw will have to go around it, too.

Even more important than matching design to use, however, is flotation. The heavier you are and the fluffier the snow is, the more flotation you need to keep you from sinking knee or hip deep; and flotation is a function of both snowshoe area and density of the lacing. Clearly you do not want the added weight of a shoe that is larger than you need, but my feeling is that the weight-to-area charts I've seen are on the conservative side. I weigh 145 and have used a 10-by-56-inch Alaskan shoe for many years. For most snow conditions I meet in Maine, it is quite ideal; but if I were traveling farther north in consistently colder, drier snow and with a pack, I might well need a larger shoe with finer lacing in the center section. Hurley and Osgood and the Faber Company both recommend a 10-by-46-inch Alaskan for someone my weight. If their recommendations are slightly conservative, those of Sherpa, Inc., the manufacturers of an aluminum-framed, neoprene-filled shoe, are just plain absurd. Sherpa claims someone weighing up to 175 pounds can use its 8-by-26-inch Featherweight shoe on flat or hilly terrain. Don't you believe it! You'll sink up to your chin in boreal frost snow. For wind-packed snow or hard crust on a mountain top, the conditions for which the Sherpa was originally developed, that claim may be close to correct.

The point is: Take all charts with a grain of salt and, if possible, experiment with some borrowed or rented shoes before you buy. Calculate the square inches of the shoe, and if you need more flotation, get a larger one. Trial runs with borrowed shoes will also give you a chance to see what style is most comfortable for you.

When it comes to materials, I much favor the traditional wooden-framed shoes. The aluminum-framed Sherpa with its claw binding has its specialized place as a mountaineer's assault shoe, but I do not like it for all-around woodland snowshoeing. Wooden-framed shoes are available in a far greater range of sizes and styles and are much more versatile.

Rawhide is the traditional webbing material, and it is still the lacing you'll see most often. Wet, springtime snow is its great enemy, however, and if it gets wet it will sag and eventually break. Neoprene is a maintenance-free material that is impervious to water and is therefore a good choice if you have to travel a lot in soggy snow. Nylon cord, which comes in a variety of diameters, is a third alternative. Fine cord, or sometimes a heavy monofilament fishing line, is often used in the toe and heel sections of the shoe and a heavier nylon cord in the center section. I recently had my pickerel shoes refilled with nylon. The performance in dry snow is excellent, and I've heard good reports about nylon's durability. But wet snow clings tenaciously to the nylon cord, packing and loading the shoes so much that they become too heavy to pick up.

Finally, one of the greatest favors a snowshoer can do himself or herself is to wear Indian-style winter moccasins. They are warm and lightweight, and unlike heavy shoepacs or hiking boots or Mickey Mouse boots, they are easy on the webbing. They are, of course, strictly cold-weather footwear. In wet snow, they quickly soak through. But in cold, powder snow and used with a simple thong or lampwick binding, also of Indian design, they'll make you feel as though you and your snowshoes are floating on air. Well, almost.

Snowshoe Sources and Information

Faber and Company, Inc., 180 Boulevard de la Riviere, C.P. 100, Loretteville, Quebec G2B 3W6, Canada, (418) 842-8476, offers the largest selection of sizes and designs of traditional snowshoes in North America that I'm aware of. A major outlet in the United States is Labonville, RR 1, Berlin, New Hampshire 03570, (603) 752-4030. A good all-purpose shoe is Faber's heavy-duty, Maine model. It is available in four sizes, numbers 11 through 14 in Faber's catalog, that range from 12-by-42 inches to 16-by-44 and retail from about $56 to $67. Call or write Faber to locate dealers in your area.

Northwoods Snowshoes, P.O. Box 5005 T.A., Denver, Colorado 80217, 800-433-6506, also has a fairly extensive range of styles and sizes with either rawhide or neoprene lacing. A 12-by-48-inch Michigan model goes for $81 in rawhide, $84.25 in neoprene.

Vermont Tubbs, Forestdale, Vermont 05745, 800-327-7026, builds a sturdy shoe available with either rawhide or neoprene webbing. L. L. Bean, Inc., Freeport, Maine 04033, 800-221-4221, and other sporting goods and hardware stores nationwide carry Vermont Tubbs shoes, or you can order directly from the company. Tubbs' wooden-frame line is limited to five models.

There are many independent craftspeople making snowshoes, too, and if there's a good snowshoemaker in your neighborhood, support him or her. Carl Heilmann, Box 213A, Route 8, Brant Lake, New York 12815, 518-494-3072, makes traditional patterns as well as wooden-framed mountaineering shoes. His carefully hand-crafted shoes draw deservedly higher prices than factory-produced ones.

The one book every snowshoe buff has to have is *Making the Attikamek Snowshoe* by Henri Vaillancourt. Order directly from the publisher, the Trust for Native American Cultures and Crafts, P.O. Box 142, Greenville, New Hampshire 03048, $27 postpaid. This book's primary purpose is to document in detail the snowshoemaking skills of the Attikamek people, who live on the headwaters of the St. Maurice River in central Quebec. It is not a "how-to" book, but you can learn how to build your own snowshoes from it. It also contains practical information on Indian snowshoe footwear and bindings.

Two old standby publications are *The Snowshoe Book* by William Osgood and Leslie Hurley (Lexington, Mass.: The Stephen Greene Press, 3d ed., 1983), paperback, $8.95 and *Snowshoeing* by Gene Prater (Seattle, Washington: The Mountaineers, 2d ed., 1980), paperback, $7.95, also available as a hardback for $14 from Peter Smith, Publisher, Inc., Magnolian, Massachusetts 01930. Both provide an introduction to snowshoes, bindings, accessories, clothing, and technique, from an eastern and western perspective respectively.

Sleeping on Air

Only a week after he had stumbled upon the New World back in 1492, Columbus saw the natives of the Bahamas using hammocks. Western Civilization has, in other words, been aware of the hammock for nearly half a millennium, but have we come to a true appreciation of the hammock in all that time? Have we given it the place of honor in our culture that it so richly deserves? No, we have not. It even took us English speakers the best part of three centuries to decide how we wanted to spell it. One variant that the *Oxford English Dictionary* lists is *hammacho,* which is, I assume, a hammock especially designed for large, muscular, hairy-chested men. And then there is the *amack* or *hammok* for folks so eager to get into their hammocks that they run hammok or amack, as the case may be.

Granted, hammocks have become a staple in lawn-and-garden stores and catalogues. It's quite all right to own one, but you don't want to get caught using it too much. After all, we Americans are an energetic, industrious folk. We have things to do and places to go. Summer is a busy time in the country. If you spend it lolling around in a hammock with a beer cooler at your elbow, the weeds will run away with your garden; you won't get your hay in; you won't have next year's wood worked up. We who live in northern climes cannot lounge year round in perpetual sunshine, so we shun the hammock even in those months when we could be enjoying its airy embrace. The hammock, our consciences tell us, is the enemy of a house that should be painted, the fence that has to be repaired, the barn that ought to be built.

Well, I have met the enemy, and I am hers. *La hamaca* is graceful, beautiful, practical. To lie suspended in the delicate but incredibly strong web of a Yucatan hammock is to experience effortless flight, to feel upheld in the hands of the air. Like skis, canoes, and sails, the hammock is one of those brilliantly simple inventions that put us in the closest possible touch with earth, air, or water at the same time that they serve utilitarian ends. In the Yucatan, where my favorite hammock comes from, hammocks are not the province merely of the loafing oaf who should be mowing the lawn but are truly utilitarian, taking the place of beds, couches, and chairs; and it is hard to imagine a lighter, more portable, more versatile piece of furniture.

Exactly where the hammock was invented way back in pre-Columbian times is not clear. Even hammock authority Denison Andrews, who wrote about the only book on hammocks I've been able to find (*How to Make Your Own Hammock and Lie in It*, New York: Workman Publishing Co., 1973, unfortunately out of print), can't offer a more precise location for the hammock's origins than "somewhere between southern Brazil and central Mexico."

The earliest hammocks were woven from the bark of the hamack tree, and not too long ago the Mayans still wove hammocks out of sisal fibers that they softened by rubbing against their thighs. Cotton is the preferred fiber now, and each Yucatan hammock is in effect a large net of finely woven cotton strands. The weave is yielding and springy yet, I am told, so strong that a large Yucatan hammock can support a Volkswagen Beetle. But this weave has other virtues besides strength, virtues that alternative hammock materials (cloth and rope) lack. Because the interstices in rope hammocks are quite large and the material heavy, you will, if you lie in the hammock in a bathing suit, take on the imprint of the hammock and stand up looking and feeling something like a waffle. Also, your beer bottle may slip through the large gaps. A cloth hammock has just the opposite failings. Its weave is so tight that it does not permit the air circulation from below that is desirable for a hot-weather bed. The naval hammock, in which the sailors of Europe dangled between decks for about three centuries, was made of canvas and was more torture device than bed. Where a true hammock is wide, airy, and sprawly, the naval hammock was small, sweaty, and cramped. Each sailor was allowed a space only 14 inches wide, and a whole crew asleep must have looked something like a bunch of bats hanging upside down from the roof of a cave. During engagements, the hammocks were rolled up tight and jammed into racks on the ship's gunwales as protection against small-arms fire. The ventilation provided by a few bullet holes would certainly have improved them.

The Yucatan hammock, by contrast, gives you the best of all possible worlds. The weave is fine enough to provide support for every square inch of you, yet it is so porous that the faintest breath of air will pass through it. Also, the netting is both so yielding and so strong that by shifting your position in the hammock, you can make it support you firmly for sitting, lounging, or sleeping. If you lie across it diagonally, for instance, you can lie as flat as you can on a firm mattress, completely free of the hammock sag and the bent back you get lying along the axis of a cloth hammock. The Yucatan hammock is also very stable because you practically sink into it. I can't imagine what kind of contortions you would have to go through to flip yourself out of it. Because it does not have the wooden spreaders used on rope hammocks, it can be rolled up into a small bundle and tucked under your arm, stuffed in a pack, or stowed in your car. The large double size I have weighs only about 4 pounds compared to about 13 pounds for a cotton rope hammock of similar size. Finally, Yucatan hammocks can be had in a natural beige or in any number of bright colors and color combinations that can make you feel you're sleeping not only on air but in the curve of an inverted rainbow as well.

Where to Find Them

The place to go for Yucatan hammocks is:

HANGOUTS
2888 Bluff Street, No. 312
Boulder, Colorado 80301
800-HANGOUT or
303-442-2533
Hangouts offers an extensive selection of hammocks in different sizes and colors and at different prices. A babies and kids' hammock, which can also double as a hanging chair for adults, goes for $18. At the opposite end of the scale is the Super Giant ($88), which could probably accommodate all the Marx Brothers at once. There are four other sizes and prices in between, and the hammocks can be ordered in solid colors, two colors, or three or more colors. Because these hammocks are all hand made, the individual weavers can indulge their fancy with colors and patterns; and no two multicolored hammocks will be exactly alike.

The standard Hangouts hammock has an all-cotton bed with nylon end strings, but for a 50 percent price increase, the bed, too, can be had in nylon. The nylon is tougher and more weather and mildew resistant, but it is nowhere near as comfortable as cotton, and with reasonable care, a cotton hammock will last many years. In other words, the gain in durability does not offset the sacrifice in comfort and the greater cost.

Smith and Hawken, 25 Corte Madera, Mill Valley, California 94941, 415-383-2000, carries one size—the double, either natural or multicolored—for $39.

The Pawleys Island hammock is the classic rope hammock. It is available in both cotton rope and polyester, but here too the gain in durability with the synthetic is not a good tradeoff for the loss of cotton's comfort, a point reflected in the fact that the venerable Pawleys Island Hammock Company of Pawleys Island, South Carolina, makes and sells many more cotton hammocks than polyester ones. Unlike cheaper imitations that use plastic spreaders,

Pawleys Island hammocks have spreaders of varnished oak. Sizes: single (48-by-80-inch bed), large (54-by-82-inch bed), and deluxe (60-by-84-inch bed). Retail prices for the cotton hammocks are about $95 for the single, about $105 and $115 for the large and deluxe. To locate a Pawleys Island dealer near you, call the company at 800-845-0311.

A high-quality hammock using a fine, soft polypropylene rope (not the hard, scratchy polypro sold in most stores) is the Twin Oaks, made in three sizes: small (48-by-82-inch bed, $63), medium (54-by-82-inch bed, $69), and large (60-by-84-inch bed, $75). Add $6 for shipping and $5 for hanging hardware. The rope joints in a Twin Oaks hammock are heat welded rather than knotted, a process possible only with a synthetic rope and one that produces a beautifully finished hammock. You can order directly from Twin Oaks, Louisa, Virginia 23093, 703-894-5126. Pier One Imports is the major nationwide retailer for Twin Oaks hammocks, though you will find them at other retail outlets as well.